Cheaper Than Therapy

How to Forgive and Overcome Anger, Anxiety, Fear and Stress

Mykey Robinson

First Published in the United Kingdom by Mykey Robinson

www.mykeyrobinson.com

Printed by CreateSpace, An Amazon.com Company

Special thanks to my friends who kept me going when I didn't know I could do it:

Dan, Tori, Jono, Michelle, Mel B, Jenks, Hanisah.

I wrote this book to give away and bless others. Once you have read it, please carry others in your thoughts that you think this book will benefit.

For information on how to run a book club for your friends, go to mykeyrobinson.com. If you have any feedback, either a testimony, or constructive criticism, I'd love to hear it. Please send emails to mykey@mykeyrobinson.com.

Contents

Introduction   7

Section 1: What is Forgiveness and Why Should We Forgive?

Chapter 1: FAQ's   13

Chapter 2: Know Your Destination   21

Chapter 3: Why Forgive? Falling In Forgiveness   31

Chapter 4: Heart vs. Head   47

Section 2: How To Forgive

Chapter 5: The Debt   57

Chapter 6: Measuring the Mark - Who to Forgive   71

Chapter 7: The Forgiveness Method   85

Section 3: How To Reconcile

Chapter 8: Hope, Fear & Clarity   101

Chapter 9: The Step Beyond Forgiveness   113

Chapter 10: Making The First Move   121

Conclusion   133

References   134

<u>WARNING:</u>

Reading this book will be HARD!

It may be painful, as you will be forced to confront painful memories.

> - You will find a million different distractions to avoid painful memories.
> - You may feel the pull back towards old habits you use to numb the pain, such as old destructive behaviours.
> - You will want to put it down or give it away.
> - You will use any and every excuse to avoid it.

UNLESS...

You have a **STRONG MOTIVATION**. This means:

> - Having a very specific and powerful reason to commit to reading
> - Getting people you trust to keep you accountable.
> - Learning to face pain rather than avoid it.

Keeping these in mind will help you to **NOT GIVE UP!**

Introduction:

Sticks and Stones May Break Your Bones But Words Will Often Hurt You

Dealing With Anger, Anxiety, Fear and Stress

There is a difference between a symptom and a cause. When we can see it or feel it physically, we can often tell the difference. Say I trip over and I put my arm out as I hit the ground. I hear a "crack" and feel pain shoot up my arm, and then notice that my arm is bent back in a very unnatural way. It's obvious that I've broken my arm and need an x-ray and medical treatment immediately.

If only it were as easy when it came to emotional issues. If only we could just take one look in the mirror and diagnose exactly what is causing our issues. We would be able to just treat them, and move on. Unfortunately, most negative emotional trials we face are neither easy to diagnose nor straightforward to treat.

Many people go through life with untreated emotional wounds. Instead of dealing with the cause, they just medicate the symptoms or ignore them altogether.

Anger, Anxiety, Fear and Stress can be root symptoms of deeper emotional wounds that need to be treated. Learning how to forgive is like emotional first aid. You'll not only learn to treat your past pains in a way that they stop affecting you now, but you'll be given a tangible process to handle any new lemons life may deal you. In the same way first aiders learn how to assess the situation, and then treat the problem, you too will learn a process that is practically applicable to the challenges life throws at us every day.

No Magic Bullets

If you are looking for a quick fix, which will change your life overnight, then this isn't it. As with most things that get right down to the root cause, it will take time and effort. Most people start to see results after a month or two of applying the steps on a daily basis. As with most behaviour changing methods, altering the way we think takes time, but the investment is often worth it.

Anger

Essentially, anger is hardwired into us and most other animals, courtesy of our "fight or flight" response. Anger is a negative emotion often caused as a result of injustice. In turn, we may seek revenge or "payback" – either physically and/or emotionally. Sometimes this anger is expressed, sometimes it is internalized, but always, whether we remember it or not, comes from somewhere. Anger isn't either good or bad. It is completely natural and simply is what it is. It's what we do with that anger and how we deal with it that is important and can be tragically destructive when it's directed in the wrong way.

Apart from making others feel bad, and often ourselves, what anger does is it can affect both our quality of life and decision making. Anger can cause us to make rash, emotional decisions which we later regret and can affect our lives in a negative way. It can sometimes even create a cycle where we get angry about this, and make further bad decisions, which we then repeat over and over until our life is in tatters and we are completely stuck in what seems like an endless cycle.

Forgiveness is a circuit breaker. It helps us to stop the spiral, and make decisions based on facts and rationale, rather than emotions like fear and anger.

Fear

Fear is closely related to anger. Both are an emotional response triggered by something that happened in our past. Fear is useful in protecting us from being hurt again. The problem here is that it can also impact us negatively via stress and poor decision making. Whereas anger inspires us to take huge risks and make poor life choices, fear can cause us to delay or fail to make a decision, and a bad one if we do! Fear can obscure our perspective, and cause us a whole lot of unnecessary stress.

Anxiety

Anxiety is non-specific fear. It is simply fear without knowing the cause. So by our definition, it is a symptom that we are yet to find the cause for. Say for example you have a fear of fans. You're not sure why, but you have this illogical fear of them. Then one day your mother reminds you of the time you stuck your finger in a fan and broke your finger. Your anxiety has just transformed into a fear.

Stress

Not all stress is bad, but too much of the wrong type is. Stress can be caused by overwork, dysfunctional relationships, lifestyle choices, health factors such as sleep and diet to name a few. A certain level of stress can be healthy, keeping us on our toes, productive and focused. But too much, and it can become unhealthy.

One factor that can cause a lot of stress is carrying emotional burdens around like anger, anxiety, fear, grudges etc. If we can reduce unhealthy stress by lessening and removing these negative emotions, we'll make better decisions, and enjoy life a heck of a lot more too.

My Story

I always suspected I had a few issues I needed to work through emotionally. I had lots I needed to sort out, but it never got bad enough that I had to see a counsellor. I did a pretty good job of ignoring it for a few years.

But I knew it was affecting me negatively in work, in love and in big life decisions. I couldn't have said exactly how though. This went on for the most part of my twenties (a time where I should have been enjoying life!).

Even if I did want to work things through, I had no idea of how, or what was causing it. It could have been any number of things: my relationship with my parents growing up, bad breakups, or the hard time I had at school. Even if I could have been specific, I didn't know what I needed to do. I had an itch I couldn't scratch; I had an itch but didn't know where.

It all changed when I started learning how to forgive. After experiencing a bad breakup and the resulting anger, anxiety, fear, and stress in 2009, I attended a few forgiveness related courses and counselling sessions. During this process, I started feeling a freedom and peace as never before. Life generally just got better. I went on to devote a significant proportion of my time to learning as much as I could about forgiveness, from experts past and present, and then applying these lessons to everyday situations in my own life and then to the lives of others.

I began looking for a simple, practical guide addressing the problems I had encountered (and was now helping others with) that was applicable to everyday situations. I figured surely someone had written a quality book on the subject. Mostly, what I found were long-winded tales of woe that depressed as much as they inspired me. I didn't find a usable, step-by-step guide among them. Most of them just ended up irritating me, as they were overly simplistic and condescending. If you're looking for a comprehensive, specific guide for overcoming an emotional problem you know only too well, then this is it.

As I applied and shared the things I was learning with others, I noticed there were a number of steps that seemed to repeat themselves over and over. Once I began using them, I got even more breakthrough. People kept coming across my path that needed help – I often found myself writing down tips on napkins and the like.

I got sick of writing on napkins. So I bought some paper… and wrote a book.

I now share these steps wherever I go – in hospitals, counselling sessions and groups. I have collected and applied many of the best psychological research studies, and completed a number of courses on the subject, then boiled them down to their essence, simplified them to make them functional, practical and able to be used in everyday situations. As I started learning how to forgive people who hurt me and then helping others apply them, I watched them experiencing the same results.

What Can You Expect In This Book?

Essentially, forgiveness is a means to an end, not an end in itself. If the whole point was to forgive, it really wouldn't give us much incentive. But there are massive benefits that come with real forgiveness. If we can forgive, we have the opportunity to gain access to these benefits.

If we can forgive, we will be able to trust again. If we can trust again, we open ourselves up to the chance of loving again. Although this isn't covered in depth, the giving and receiving of love is essential for us to live fuller lives, without which we may feel broken, hurt, alienated or all three. The belief that makes a person believe that they are somehow, 'unlovable', is the most common cause of brokenness I have seen. If you can learn how to experience love again, it often goes toward rectifying this situation.

Contents of The Book?

The Book is divided into 3 sections:

Section 1: What Is Forgiveness and Why Should we forgive?

In the first section we'll look at what forgiveness is, and why we need to do it. In Chapters 1 and 2, we define and clarify what forgiveness is, and set some clear goals and definitions of what it looks like when we succeed. In Chapter 3 our focus is on finding the motivation to forgive. Having a clear motivation is the most important element in forgiving, without which, we're just fooling ourselves. In Chapter 4, we look at the difference between our hearts and heads, and understand the importance of getting them to work together.

Section 2: How To Forgive

Chapters 5, 6 and 7 lay out a practical step-by-step forgiveness process. We look at how people owe us "debts", and what to do to permanently get rid of these. We look at how underlying assumptions sometimes need to be understood and altered for us to learn how to trust again, and the different types of relationships that owe us different types of debts.

Section 3: How To Reconcile

In Chapter 8, we look at how we often need to assess the risks of reconciling with a person, types of abuse, how to tell whether they're genuinely repentant, and the factors to consider when seeking justice. In Chapters 9 and 10, we look at how to approach people to seek reconciliation and how to increase our chances of success if and when we want it to happen.

There are exercises at the end of each chapter. I encourage you to do them with a friend if you can. The case studies in this book are inspired by real people - However, names and situations have been tweaked to protect their identities.

Section 1:
What is Forgiveness
and Why Should We Do It?

Chapter 1: FAQ's

Real Forgiveness is the way we can rid ourselves of our baggage, for good.

In a past life I worked at an airport, and here I witnessed many unbelievable things happen during that time. One of the more interesting cases I saw was of a mother and son who arrived after spending an arduous 96 hours in transit. They'd flown from Russia to Los Angeles via Western Europe, slept the night in a park in downtown L.A, then hopped on another flight to Sydney the next day.

After touching down, they got through passport checks, and placed their hand luggage on the x-ray machines. When asked to open one of their backpacks, they refused vehemently. The customs official opened the bag and the head of a live Chihuahua popped out. The bag had avoided detection at 4 airports, and been on 3 long haul flights with them in the cabin. The mother and son duo said they'd spent their life savings getting to Australia and wanted to apply for refugee asylum.

Tragically, quarantine officials told them the dog would have to be put down if they stayed in Australia as it couldn't stay. The pair deliberated long and hard, and then asked to be transported home.

Many people are as attached and protective of their old emotional wounds as our Russian travellers were with their hand luggage. They believe they've worked through their past, but at some point it pops up again in their lives, like a Chihuahua in a rucksack. They may feel that they have their life under control, but really, there's a missing piece. They might suspect they have emotional baggage but they're cluttered emotionally and/or spiritually and they don't know what to do about it.

Others are only too aware they have emotional issues. They eat, breathe and sleep with it on their minds, and have tried plenty of times to rid themselves of the issues. They may take medication for it – to sleep, feel happy or less stressed. They may have had therapy with limited success but they still have no idea what to do about it.

People aren't born with baggage. Somewhere along the line it is thrust upon them. Often, it starts in childhood - it did for me. It's easy for it to become assimilated into a person's identity, into the fabric of a person's livelihood – to the point that they believe it's a part of them and surrender any hope of overcoming it. To these people, I say the following: If you were not born with it, you acquired it. If it was acquired, it can be un-acquired. How many depressed new-born babies have you seen lately?

Emotional Baggage – Who Cares?

I travel light. Always have. In fact, I could pack my life into a suitcase and take off in a few hours. I try to keep my emotional life in the same state, but this takes effort. It's so easy to acquire clutter. I have to regularly prune back my "stuff" so I can remain in a state of readiness for what each day may bring. If I don't regularly pare away unnecessary clutter in my life, it's harder to find stuff that I actually need, and it becomes more stressful. Keeping too much unnecessary stuff is called hoarding. It clogs every available space and gets in the way of living life.

In the same manner, we can also fall victims to hoarding emotional baggage as a product of holding onto past wounds. Every day is filled with potential emotional hazards – whether it is stress, emotional hurt, or rejection, and each time they take a hold in our lives, we acquire another which adds weight to pile what we are already carrying around: It's like death by a thousand cuts.

Most people have emotional baggage, whether they're aware of it or not. It is almost universal to the human condition to have painful memories that cause us to experience fear, anxiety, stress and anger. If we can get rid of these side effects, we'll be able to make good decisions with improved clarity.

It's what people do with their baggage that matters. A person can really only do one of two things with it:

- Carry it all around with them or
- Let it go

Some people think that they can nurse every hurt, and hold grudges for their whole lives. In reality, this isn't an option. There is an increasing amount of evidence pointing to the fact that holding onto bad experiences as such, not only results in worse physical and emotional health, but it also negatively affects relationships[1]. In the past, forgiveness was almost exclusively left to those in religious institutions, however, in the last thirty or so years, a branch of clinical research has sprung up, called 'Forgiveness Therapy'. These researchers have unearthed a number of surprising findings on the benefits and applications of forgiveness. This book is the application of these, as well as my own findings, to our everyday lives.

However enticing holding onto your hurts may be, does it really help? At the very least, it's not the most practical option. As with physical baggage, there are items a person can choose to hang onto for a time – perhaps for comfort or dependence. Perhaps they are afraid that they'll fall apart if they let it go. There are many reasons it becomes necessary to let go of baggage – it's become too heavy to carry, or it is no longer necessary etc.

This book is about learning the art of letting go.

Successfully dealing with emotional baggage is foundational to living life to the full– it will have a far greater impact on a person's future than they might think. Research[2] shows that letting go of baggage results in feeling:

- Less hurt and angry
- Less stressed
- Less depressed
- Less distrusting
- More hopeful and optimistic
- More compassionate
- More self confident
- More trusting
- More loving and loveable
- More healthy

So How Do I Let Go?

One way of permanently letting go of your emotional baggage is by Forgiving. Many researchers call it "Forgiveness Therapy", but the rudimentary concept has been around for millennia throughout various religious teachings and philosophies.

Forgiveness takes place in the heart through the cancelling of debts. Willingness is an essential ingredient - it is ineffective unless your heart is in it - where there is real "heartfelt" forgiveness.

Forgiveness is an art form, not a science, much like falling in love. In the same way people improve as they practice an artistic ability, they can get better at forgiving too, and maximise their chances of success. In 'Cheaper Than Therapy', I lay out a simple, practical method that I personally use to forgive to stay emotionally clutter-free. I've seen great success with it on myself and other people.

It is a practical, step-by-step guide to get free of emotional baggage, forgive past experiences and live life to the full today. I have seen victims of sexual abuse set free, 'rageaholics' discover more peace than they ever thought possible, people freed from clinical depression and suicidal thoughts, and relationships restored which seemed beyond hope. All of these people live fuller, happier lives than they did before.

But What If I Don't Want To Forgive?

You may feel that forgiveness is not an option for one of three reasons:

- You Can't Forgive
- You Don't Want To Forgive
- You Don't Need to Forgive

You Can't Forgive

Not all people have experienced massive trauma in their lives, but I have seen people who were able to forgive their perpetrators 100%. If they can, it must at least be possible for the rest of us.

The size of hurt is closely related to the time it takes to forgive, but the most critical factor can be the person who was hurt, as some people seem to possess a greater predisposition towards forgiving than others. Most of the time, it's not that people don't want to forgive; rather they just can't repeatedly take the pain over and over again. Perhaps you may not have found a way to fully forgive something or someone, leading you to believe that it is simply not possible to forgive completely.

You Don't Want To Forgive

Finding the motivation to forgive is essential. The ability to forgive has more to do with the predisposition of the person doing the forgiving rather than the scale of the harm done.

Personality traits which impact directly on a person's ability to forgive include empathy, narcissism, a strong sense of justice, age, beliefs, and aversion to pain, among others. The first step in changing a "can't" into a "can", is finding a motivation that works for you. Without it, people can take far longer to forgive.

You Don't Need To Forgive

A lot of people are unaware that they need forgiveness in some part of their lives. Most people are not completely aware of what is going on within their own hearts and minds. To rectify this, the place to start is to look at where they feel angry, anxious, afraid or sad, where these emotions stem from is where the answer is. When you cannot trust a person or find a particular type of relationship hard, begin by looking at why and where you first learned this.

The most common response I hear is "I don't need to forgive". If you've lived in this world for very long, you will understand that being hurt is part of being human; it's how you respond that sets you apart. When people tell me they don't need to forgive I figure they're either in complete denial that they experience emotional pain (and may be using something to numb it) or they're emotionally ignorant (often this is the case with guys).

Is There a Difference Between Forgiveness and Reconciliation?

Forgiveness is a means to an end, rather than an end in itself. The goal of forgiveness is to instil a new ability to trust and have faith in relationships. As people learn to trust again, they make it possible to experience love once more – in similar relationships and situations – and even perhaps at some point with the person who originally hurt them. Forgiveness and reconciliation is not the same thing, contrary to popular belief.

Forgiveness: The goal of forgiveness is for us to no longer feel anger at the people who caused the hurt. Rather than repressing and pretending like it's not there anymore, there is genuinely no anger felt towards them. Anger can be a healthy emotion (fight or flight is a natural self-protective response), but when it hangs around unaddressed for too long, it can become destructive.

Reconciliation: No contact whatsoever is required with this person for this to happen. With reconciliation, the goal is to reach a place where someone who has been hurt can again trust the person who did it. Even if you can, the question still remains as to whether you should reconcile (which is addressed later on). Practically, when people start to see these two factors, they're making progress:

The Negative

- The degree to which they keep hold of a grudge
- How they withdraw from the relationship
- Their desire to avenge or punish the person they blame (including themselves).

The Positive

- Their readiness to forgive, or grant pardon for emotional debts owed.
- The empathy they feel towards the offender

What's In It For Me If I Do Forgive?

Forgiveness is proven to have many positive health and psychological side effects. There is a large body of evidence showing that complete forgiveness:

- Reduces anxiety
- Reduces depression
- Increases self-esteem
- Improves marital relationships
- Improves physical health
- Decreases guilt
- Decreases shame
- Decreases psychosomatic illnesses
- Improves quality of friendships

Anxiety disorders affect almost 20% of America's population, and almost one in ten experiencing depression each year[3], and the World Health Organization shows that anxiety is one of the most commonly reported disorders in most western countries[4]. If forgiveness can offer even temporary relief for some of these symptoms then it is worth giving it a try.

Chapter 1 Exercises

Answer all questions honestly - there are no wrong answers; write them in your notebook. You will have important insights when you least expect it, so have it on you at all times.

1. Set a definite date by which you will read this book and commit to it.

2. What is the main motive behind you reading this book?

3. What do you want to improve/get better at, as a result?

4. Think of one relationship role you want to improve at. Express it in terms of "I want to be a better (mum/boyfriend/son/friend etc.)". Journal exactly what this will look like, how will the people involved change/ feel as a result?

5. List any other aspects you want to improve.

6. Think of at least two people you can ask to keep you accountable, encourage you, and kick your butt when you're procrastinating. Contact them in the next twenty-four hours.

7. What penalty or reward will aid in motivating you to finish this book? Commit to doing this.

8. How long will it take me to read a chapter? Who can keep me accountable to this goal?

9. What reward can I give myself at the end of each chapter, and for finishing the book?

Chapter 2: Know Your Destination

We first have to know what it looks like to know when we have found it.

A famous U.S. senator embarked on a train leaving from New York City. When asked to produce his ticket by an inspector, he tried in vain to find it. As he turned out his pockets, he muttered to himself "I must find that ticket."

The inspector, who stood waiting beside him said, "Don't worry about it, sir. I recognize you. We know you had a ticket. Just mail it to the railroad operator when you find it."

"That's not what's troubling me", replied the senator, "I need to find it to know where I'm going."

Common Misunderstandings of Forgiveness

We need to know where we're going before we decide how to get there, or we might misunderstand what forgiving looks like, even if we may have a vague idea of what it means. It is essential to make it very clear what it is and isn't, so we know when we're approaching our destination.

The two most common misunderstandings are:

> 1: We do it primarily in our heads, not our hearts.

> 2: It's what a person did to us that we must forgive.

It's important to be very clear about what forgiveness isn't, before we can know what it is to ensure there are no misunderstandings and remove our (conscious and subconscious) reservations about exactly what it is that we're doing.

Forgiveness Isn't...

Forgiveness Isn't Reconciling

In many circumstances people are hurt by those closest to them. It's hard to continue to relate to them, but in many cases it's a necessity. It's a common belief and misconception that forgiving means being a doormat, thereby exposing you to further abuse. The fact is forgiveness is actually different to reconciliation. Full forgiveness can happen without reunification with the person(s) who hurt you. This is why we look at forgiving before we look at how to reconcile. Forgiveness only requires one party - you. Reconciling is where we decide to include another party in the process. Ideally, it's best to forgive before you try and reconcile, but unfortunately, few of us live in an ideal world.

Forgiveness Isn't Condoning

We are not saying that a person's actions are okay by forgiving, nor are we condoning them in any way. If we have a strong sense of justice, we may feel that we can't allow a person to get away with an act that is clearly wrong. We are not approving of what they may have done. Bringing them to justice is still an option, but it's best left until after we have begun the process of forgiving them.

Forgiveness Isn't Excusing or Justifying

We are not excusing or justifying their actions - however difficult or unfair their life was. It is completely irrelevant to the person doing the forgiving, and should remain so. Just like an honest accountant, the forgiver mustn't give any discounts when writing off a debt but must fully attribute it to the person at fault.

> ### The Buck Stops With You
> *Growing up, John was abused both physically and verbally by his father. John's father experienced almost identical treatment at the hands of his own father (John's grandfather). For many years John didn't feel that he could attribute any blame to his father, as all that his father had known growing up was abuse too. By not doing this, John inadvertently minimised what his dad owed him. The first step for John on the journey to permanently ridding himself of his significant baggage was recognising it was necessary to fully lay responsibility at his dad's feet, even though he still loved him. In doing this, he made a full accounting of what his dad never gave him, but should have.*

Forgiveness Isn't Pardoning

Forgiveness is not letting someone off from the consequences for their actions. Deciding on a course of action to get justice is separate to forgiving someone. Factors involved with this issue are addressed in a later chapter. Although part of this process involves overcoming the desire for revenge, it may be that justice needs to be done to prevent it happening again. We're not giving anyone a free pass – we will still need to work through the fallout.

Forgiveness Isn't Forgetting

In many situations it can be dangerous to forget what a person has done in the past, as it can mean exposing yourself to a repeat of what they did previously. However, if the other person is genuinely sorry (usually demonstrated by a change in behaviour), it may be that they can be forgiven without this happening. The question is: How do we work out when they're genuine? This is discussed in chapter 8.

Forgiveness Isn't Weak

Some people will tell you that expressing your anger is the best way to get over past hurts - to get angry and get even. We have been conditioned by Hollywood to think that "payback" is the heroic option, but immature children are just as capable of "tit for tat" as hard Hollywood heroes. Acknowledging and expressing anger are two different things.

Anger is a part of the process, and it is important to recognise and acknowledge that you feel it. Anger in and of itself isn't either good or bad. It simply is what it is. It's what we do with that anger that is important. Anger exists in some ways as a protection mechanism to prevent further harm - "fight or flight" is a basic instinct for most mammals.

Forgiveness Isn't Easy

It's obvious, but still worth saying. Genuine, bona fide, 100% forgiveness isn't simple and neither is it straightforward. It often involves peeling back the pain, one layer at a time. Perhaps you find yourself currently mired in one of the following places:

- You just want this baggage gone, but don't know how to let it go.
- You can't put your finger on what exactly it is you need to forgive.
- You retaliated, and now things are even worse, beyond reconciliation.

In this book, we'll discover:

- The simple, practical steps to get rid of emotional baggage.
- How to make decisions unencumbered by anger, anxiety, fear and stress.
- How to get your heart and mind working together, rather than against each other.

Forgiveness Isn't Dependent on Them

Forgiveness doesn't rely on an apology, nor do we need to involve the person who hurt us. It can be done on our own, with zero input from them. It is in our self-interest to forgive, as it can lead to many life-improving benefits[5]. It doesn't matter if they are dead, have permanently disappeared, or can't be contacted. You can still permanently, once and for all, get rid of emotional baggage through forgiveness.[6]

Unforgiveness doesn't hurt the other person - it only hurts you. Imagine I run your dog over, without knowing I've done it, and just keep on driving. I don't know or care that I've hurt you. You, on the other hand, are acutely aware, and are sure to hold a grudge, and be angry and bitter about the whole affair. This grudge may end up negatively affecting your life-long term – perhaps you get stressed any time you leave your house, or cross the road. Perhaps you become depressed or experience uncontrollable anger as a result. One thing is for sure, I'm not losing any sleep over it, nor will I ever be brought to justice. Whatever they did - if the person who hurt you doesn't know or care, or can't be contacted and/or brought to justice - you can still find freedom from the burden you carry.

Overcoming Fear

Jessie's father sexually abused her growing up. From the age of 9 to 16, Jessie would be left with her drunk and out of control father. She lost count of the times she was sexually assaulted by him after her mother fled the house. One day she was hiding in the garden as he stumbled through, calling out her name. She started praying that he would die. A few weeks later he suddenly died of a heart attack.

Jessie has suffered ever since. She felt guilty and broken on the inside and it affected her marriage. Every time she visited the house she grew up in to see her mother, she would be choked by fear and would sit for up to an hour in her car, choking back tears and trying to muster the courage to go inside.

Jessie didn't think she could ever entirely move on from what her father did to her now that he was dead, as she would never be able to confront him, or see him brought to justice. When she realized that her freedom was completely independent of him, Jessie began to forgive her mother, father, and herself.

One day she was visiting the house she grew up in. It was only after she got to the front door that she realized she hadn't been afraid at all. She knew from that point on that she was different, and was going to stay that way.

Definition: Forgiveness is

According to Webster's Third Edition, to forgive is:

- To cease to feel resentment against, on accord of wrong committed
- To give up claim to requital from or retribution upon an offender, to absolve; pardon.[7]

Cancelling a Debt

The best definition of Forgiveness I have seen is "to cancel a debt or payment". When someone hurts you, they create an unpaid debt. Our desire for revenge or retribution is us attempting to have this debt repaid, the voice that says "go on, get them back. They have it coming".

Although forgiveness can be difficult to define, there are three elements that consistently appear in psychological literature:

> 1: Regaining a more balanced and compassionate view of the offender and the event (Putting it in perspective);
> 2: Giving up the right to seek revenge or lash out at the offender (giving up desire for revenge).[8]
> 3: Decreasing negative feelings towards, and avoidance of, the offender (removing the desire for anger); and

Forgiveness Is...

Forgiveness Is An Art Form

Just like falling in love, forgiveness is an art form rather than a science. We do certain things to maximize our chances of falling in love - such as grooming, asking people out, online dating etc. In the same fashion, we can also do certain things to be more likely to forgive. In both cases, we create a far greater chance that our desired outcome will come to pass.

Even people with two left feet get better with dance lessons. However you do it, the amount of effort you put in usually reflects the results you get out. This is the case for almost all aspects of life itself! The same is true when it comes to forgiving someone; the more you do it, the better you get at it.

Forgiveness Is a Process

The forgiveness process starts with a decision to forgive (Section 1). It continues as a person gets rid of the desire for revenge (Section 2) and is complete when they have set aside all residual negative emotions such as anger, revenge, anxiety, regret, guilt, and fear to the point where they are able to consider reconciliation and/or justice (section 3).

It can also take a long time for some. For significant wounds, one study took 1 – 3 years to see full forgiveness take hold for some patients.[9] Everybody works at a different pace. Someone might take 6 months to forgive a hurt that might take years for another.

Forgiveness Is a Conscious Choice and a Lifelong Habit.

"Forgiveness is not an occasional act, it is a constant attitude."

- Martin Luther King Jr.

Forgiveness doesn't happen overnight, nor does it happen in a logical way that easily fits into a 3, 7 or 21 step process. Healing and forgiving is messy and often you don't realise how far you've come until you look back.

Sometimes it means deciding to forgive every day, over and over again until our hearts listen. We don't necessarily have to reach a place where we want to do it right away. At times it is enough to be aware that our holding onto grudges is negatively impacting our life. Sometimes you need more to reach a point where you are "willing to be willing" to forgive. In the next chapter we look at finding the motivation to forgive.

Forgiveness Is a Decision That is Entirely Yours

In a number of studies, it was found that the majority of participants believed that an apology wasn't essential for them to forgive.[10] Forgiveness is a choice on the part of the forgiver that does not depend on the offender's actions or repentance. Apologies and restitution are not critical to the forgiveness process. Sometimes it's the other party that don't necessarily want to be friends, even if they were entirely at fault, but this makes no difference.

Forgiveness Brings Clarity

Anger, anxiety and fear often get in the way of making a quality decision. We might make a rash decision from a place of anger, or fear. When we forgive past experiences, we get clarity devoid of the negative emotions that obstruct being able to see where to go from here.

Letting Go of Revenge

All revenge does is make life worse. Revenge is a cycle that leads to further entanglement and pain, and can often enslave us to further unforgiving, bitterness and destructive habits.

One research study looking at relationship satisfaction after infidelity and forgiveness, described the process of not forgiving as a destructive cycle, and forgiveness as the "short circuit" allowing you to escape it (and the accompanying permanent relationship breakdown).[11]

Say you hunt me down for running your dog over, and strangle my cat as a reprisal. I find out it was you, and I decide to drown your guinea pigs. You assassinate my goldfish as payback, so I hatch and execute a plan to end the life of your pet carpet snake. Clearly, the line of no return has been crossed, so you kill my prizewinning vulture. In the end, we'll both end up with empty zoos, and garden beds like lumpy mattresses, not to mention a gulf of bitterness and rage between us.

Hollywood churns out movies by the truckload all about revenge and retribution, but in real life, things rarely end as neatly as the conclusion to Die Hard or Rambo (although with the steady flow of sequels, will they really ever end?)

Perhaps the most famous phrase on revenge is a quote from Jesus in the bible – "an eye for an eye", (which means that if someone hits you, you get payback for that amount). In this passage, Jesus is saying that revenge isn't the solution:

"You have heard that it has been said, 'An eye for an eye and a tooth for a tooth.' But I tell you, do not fight with the man who wants to fight. Whoever hits you on the right side of the face, turn so he can hit the other side also"

- Jesus

He often exaggerated to make a point, which in this case, was on showing kindness instead of revenge, to your enemy. He wasn't condoning ongoing, habitual exploitation or abuse. It is easy to interpret forgiveness as a weak and submissive trait, where people remain trapped in abuse. Yet the point here is to act in the opposite way toward enemies than the world would – i.e. extract similar payment to what is owed. It is foolish and dangerous to expose yourself to repeated abuse. It's probably safe to assume that wasn't what Jesus meant, and yet he also promotes radical, costly, dangerous forgiveness.

Many misunderstand Jesus when he says "turn the other cheek". He isn't saying we should expose ourselves to repetitive exploitation.

It all depends on whether you are doing it out of strength or weakness. If you are trapped in a cycle of exploitation and/or abuse because you have no other option, you need help, you need someone to rescue you, and bring your oppressor to justice.

BUT, if we are in a position of strength where we could retaliate in a way that could really hurt the other person, and we choose not to - we're making a powerful statement. We are breaking the cycle of revenge and doing exactly the opposite of what the world, and our enemy would expect. Crazy, but possibly the boldest move we could make.

"An eye for an eye only ends up making the whole world blind"

- Mahatma Ghandi

Revenge and Debts

Almost universally, our initial reaction is to retaliate when someone hurts us. It is not always possible to get an "eye for an eye", but we might seek a tooth or an ear. We may choose not to confront the person face to face, but we'll extract payment in other ways – whether it is through gossip, slashed tyres, even fantasizing about hurting them. It still counts, even if you don't actually "do" anything.

When I was a teenager, I developed a rather vivid imagination. I went to a tough school, and was picked on fairly regularly being small for my age. The only way I got them back was to imagine beating them up, I would replay and tinker with various scenarios of how I would get my bullies back. This went on well into adulthood for me, until I realized how pointless and harmful it was.

When someone hurts us they create a "debt" that they owe. It's a transaction that needs to be closed before the forgiver can experience freedom. When we say, "you owe me an apology" we are unintentionally referring to this principle.

There may be debts we have forgotten, or suspect are there, but aren't sure. These debts are like shadows. Most of the time we're unaware of them, but when we are, all we can see is a vague outline.

It's difficult to know when you get to the point of being totally free of a debt, once and for all, but as you learn to recognise the debts you're owed and forgive them, you'll start to feel and react differently in familiar situations.

Our Tendency to Forgive

In one psychological study, it was found that there is a "Revenge versus Forgiveness factor" – which reflects a general tendency in people to forgive (or to seek revenge) regardless of circumstances.[12] It was found that there are a number of factors that are strongly linked to this - with age, gender, belief, and religious practice being the most significant determinants. The ability to forgive and forego revenge is most strongly associated with age than any other demographic factor because after weighing out the pros and cons, they are often the most motivated, and have the least to lose.

Investment and Motivation

When you're heavily invested in a relationship, you are more likely to forgive, because you have a vested interest in making it work. When a marriage breaks down, couples often go to therapy to try and resolve their differences. When a friendship breaks down this rarely happens, and parties go their separate ways. One could argue a big factor that motivates people to forgive is how much they have riding on a relationship, and how much they lose if it falls apart.

Not everyone has as clear a motivation as married couples. However we all need to find a clear motivation to forgive if we are to get to a point where we can live free of past anger and fear.

For some, the loss and negative effects of holding onto a grudge might be enough for some to let it go. Whereas for others, it might be coming to a place where they can empathize with the person who hurt them. Everybody needs to find a motivation that works for them if they're to find heartfelt forgiveness. The clearer it is for us, the easier the process will become.

Chapter 2 Exercises:

Answer all questions honestly - there are no wrong answers. Get a notebook and write them there...

1. Would your close friends describe you as someone who forgives easily? Would you describe yourself as a forgiving person? Why?

2. How frequently do you experience each of the below:

I sometimes get really angry with stressful situations/ people.   Yes/No
I sometimes feel really guilty   Yes/No
I sometimes feel a deep sense of shame for no clear reason   Yes/No
I sometimes feel intense fear in certain situations   Yes/No
I sometimes feel extremely optimistic about life   Yes/No
I find it easy to imagine myself in another person's situation (empathize) Yes/No
I would say I have a strong sense of self-confidence   Yes/No

3. Which of the above things would you like to change? Why? Do you have any suspicions of what might be causing this?

4. How would you rate yourself at the moment in regard to each of the below categories (1 being low, 10 being high):

Stress/Anxiety   1 2 3 4 5 6 7 8 9 10
Sadness/Depression   1 2 3 4 5 6 7 8 9 10
Guilt   1 2 3 4 5 6 7 8 9 10
Shame   1 2 3 4 5 6 7 8 9 10
Hopefulness   1 2 3 4 5 6 7 8 9 10
Self Confidence / Self-esteem   1 2 3 4 5 6 7 8 9 10
Physical Health   1 2 3 4 5 6 7 8 9 10
Romantic relationships   1 2 3 4 5 6 7 8 9 10
Compassion/empathy for others   1 2 3 4 5 6 7 8 9 10

5. Read each of the following statements. For those you disagree with write a paragraph in your notebook on why exactly this is.

Chapter 3: Why forgive? Falling In Forgiveness

To forgive, we first have to believe why we need to.

Sometimes it's beyond impossible to make yourself forgive. Forgiving is more like falling asleep, or falling in love – you can't make yourself do it, but you can make every effort to improve your chances. A group of children offered some insightful thoughts on what "falling in love" is like:

> "I think you're supposed to get shot with an arrow or something, but the rest of it isn't supposed to be so painful." (Harlen, 8)

> "If falling in love is anything like learning how to spell, I don't want to do it. It takes too long." (Leo, 7)

> "Lovers will just be staring at each other and their food will get cold. Other people care more about the food." (Brad, 8)

> "Love will find you, even if you are trying to hide from it. I have been trying to hide from it since I was five, but the girls keep finding me." (Bobby, 8)

> "Be a good kisser. It might make your wife forget that you never take out the trash." (Randy, 8)

Forgiveness can be very much like falling in love. We like the idea of it, but for some actually doing it can be a more difficult task - controlling how, who and when can be at best unpredictable, even hazardous.

Falling In Forgiveness

So how do we make ourselves forgive? Is it possible? Often, the hardest thing about forgiving is actually wanting to, and then getting your heart to agree with your head. Finding and retaining the motivation to forgive can sometimes be elusive.

You can't make forgiveness happen, but you can do many things that will help you to get in the mood. Perhaps we should call it "falling in forgiveness". In the same way you put on perfume, wear your best clothes, and groom yourself, , you can also put yourself in the best position to forgive someone.

The Ultimate Goal

One way to find the motivation to forgive is to have a clear direction of what we want to achieve. When we forgive, it always allows us to trust again. When we regain trust, we open our hearts to love in ways we couldn't before.

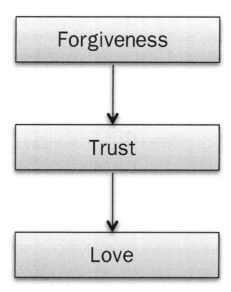

Forgiveness Lets Us Trust Again

When we are able to forgive, we will become more able to trust again. As a result, we will be able to make ourselves vulnerable in similar situations with the same person, or in a relationship of a similar nature.

If we've been cheated on, we'll find it hard to trust our next partner or the same one if we decide to reconcile. We might get irrationally suspicious when our partner spends time with others. When we get to the point where we can trust again, we will let ourselves be vulnerable with others. It takes courage to do this, which is only made possible through forgiving previous hurts first.

If you can trust, you can love

> The root of the word courage is 'cor'—the Latin word for heart. In one of its earliest forms, the word courage literally had a very different definition than it does today. Courage originally meant "To speak one's mind by telling all one's heart."
>
> - Brene Brown

Love is the ultimate goal. If we are able to provide trust, we can then be less cautious when falling in love or rekindling the broken relationship(s). Often when our walls are up we won't let love in even if we want to - we'll block it, strive for it, overcook it, and sabotage it at every point. I personally went through a long process of taking down my walls, as I had found it hard to trust in the past due to rejection. As I learned to forgive, I found sharing my feelings with people much easier.

The more we can love, the more people will reciprocate and return the love. As we come to find that we're loved, valued, appreciated, and naturally worth loving, we will find it easier to forgive other parties, and ourselves.

Learning that you're lovable is the key that will unlock your heart, and you're sure to feel happier as a result.

Keep in mind the benefits and costs

One way to find the motivation to forgive is to know that the rewards are worth the effort. To convince our hearts to completely let go of a debt and drop our baggage once and for all, we need a very clear reason for why we are doing it. Without this, we can go through the motions all we want but we still won't make any progress. Studies[13] have shown that forgiving and letting go of anger can do one or more of the following:

- Reduces anxiety
- Reduces depression
- Increases self-esteem
- Improves marital relationships
- Improves physical health
- Decreases guilt
- Decreases shame
- Decreases psychosomatic illnesses
- Improves quality of relationships

Do any of these spark your interest? Read on.

z

The Franklin Effect

Benjamin Franklin, one of the founding fathers of the U.S., was facing frequent animosity by an opposing politician in Pennsylvania who had in his library a very rare book. Franklin wrote to him, asking to borrow it for a few days. After receiving and reading it, Franklin returned it with a note expressing his deep gratitude. When they next met in parliament, the man spoke to Franklin for the first time and was ever after extremely helpful whenever asked. They actually became great friends until the man died.

Psychologists have observed this phenomenon frequently, nicknamed The Ben Franklin effect – where a person who has *done* someone a favour is more likely to do that person another one, and feel more positive about them than if they had *received* a favour from that person. Our subconscious can't handle the mismatch between our thoughts and actions (known as "cognitive dissonance"). If we're helping a person, our subconscious adjusts the value we place on them because we don't want to feel like we are helping someone who doesn't "deserve" it. When a person helps someone, the rest of them adjust to value the person accordingly. If we can somehow do the same by creating cognitive dissonance towards the person who hurt us, we'll be more likely to see value in them, and hence feel like they are worth forgiving.

Valuing People

"Try not to become a man of success. Rather become a man of value." - Albert Einstein

In most cultures, certain people are treated better than others, usually based on certain attributes. Two obvious ones include height and attractiveness. In a number of studies[14], attractive people almost always were treated better than people considered less attractive. Many societies value physical beauty highly. A "beautiful" person's worth is usually immediately obvious to the eye, so they are frequently given preferential treatment.

Before we can forgive someone, we need to believe that the person is worth forgiving. If we don't believe that another person has value, it could be hard to motivate ourselves to forgive. We need to learn how to recognise value in a person to believe they're "worth forgiving", whether they're sorry for what they've done, or not.

How do we value a person? Is it how good they are at something, how attractive they are, their sense of humour things they share in common, amount of money etc? Every person values others differently. We'll find it much easier to forgive someone whom we perceive is valuable to us. Moreover if the person is the complete opposite of everything we use to value a person, we could make the mistake of believing they have no value, and hence, are not "worth" forgiving. We can believe this about others, or ourselves.

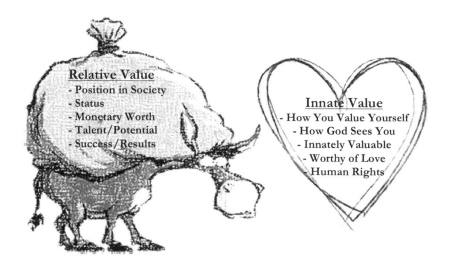

Relative Value
- Position in Society
- Status
- Monetary Worth
- Talent/Potential
- Success/Results

Innate Value
- How You Value Yourself
- How God Sees You
- Innately Valuable
- Worthy of Love
- Human Rights

Human rights are commonly defined as "inalienable fundamental rights to which a person is inherently entitled simply because she or he is a human being." The Universal Declaration of Human Rights[15] was drafted by the United Nations General Assembly as a result of the holocaust. It consisted of 30 articles that a human being is entitled to, simply because they are human. Logic follows that if humans have innate rights they must have innate value, hence even the most depraved person carries value. We may find it hard to perceive any value in a person when we think of them as being completely evil and having no redeeming features... but find value we must. We need to recognize that everyone has value, including ourselves. If we succeed in doing this, we will not be able to say that anyone is unworthy of forgiveness.

Forgiveness and addiction

In my limited personal experience with addictions, people use a substance to numb or anaesthetize emotional pain. We may discover that as we forgive, we reduce our dependency on things that keep us going. All pain has meaning, and when we feel it, rather than numbing or ignoring it, we should find the thing that is causing it, and work on it.

Forgiveness Factors

Some people are much more willing and able to forgive than others. One study[16] discovered that the tendency in people to forgive (or to seek revenge) is influenced by 4 demographic factors:

- Age: The older a person is, the more likely they are to forgive.
- Belief: People who believe in God are more likely to forgive than those who don't.
- Religious practice: Those who regularly attended church had a higher propensity to forgive rather than seek revenge (type of church was not specified).
- Gender: Women are more likely to forgive than men.

The Older You Get...

Forgiveness motivated by:

- Commitment to others
- Investment in others
- Personal needs later in life

People's priorities change as they grow older.[17] In their youth, people will often maintain wide social networks (which has increased exponentially with social networking) to achieve their aspirations and goals such as wealth, status, attractiveness, and influence. They construct a wider network of friends who they are less invested in, and who serve a specific functional purpose.

At a certain age, ambition becomes less of a concern, and people's priorities change to focus on relationships that are important to them – family and close friends with an emphasis on investing in future generations. A smaller network of relationships means a higher commitment toward each. Due to the fact that people can't easily walk away from people they have heavily invested in, they are more likely to forgive them. It can sometimes be self-motivated too, as people need care, love and assistance in old age.

Reprioritizing Relationships

David went through a mid-life crisis at 52. It lasted almost a year. He had climbed to the top of the corporate ladder, achieving every goal he set for himself. But he wasn't happy. The career he once thought would satisfy him hadn't, and his second marriage ended in divorce. It was time to take a good hard look at himself, and what was important. He found himself gravitating towards his grandchildren, wanting to spend time with them. Soon afterwards he discovered that his son had lost most of David's retirement money in a ponzi scheme. If it were anyone but his son it would have gotten really nasty. But this was the father of his grandchildren and only son, and he discovered to his surprise that staying in their lives was more important than getting the money back.

Another possibility is that the older we get, the more we think about our later years, and who will assist us when we grow old and require help in old age. The more we intend to rely on the relationship, the more we are willing to forego vengeance to retain the relationship.

To Think About:

How invested and committed are you to the relationship?
What is important to you – a wide social network, or a close group of loyal friends?

Women Empathize Better

Forgiveness motivated by:

- Sensitivity
- Empathy towards others
- Awareness of own heart and loss of relationship

Men can sometimes be less sensitive than women, often overlooking more subtle forms of communication. This also impacts a man's capacity for forgiveness. Studies[18] have found that generally, men can be less sensitive than women when it comes to dealing with hurtful events. They also found that men are more likely to choose revenge as an option than women, whereas women are more likely to apologise in similar circumstances.

The most common response I hear from men is "I don't need to forgive", whereas women are far more aware of the things going on in their hearts. Women are better equipped to let go of their emotional pain because they are more aware of the negative impacts of not forgiving on both themselves and others, and so opt for acts of revenge far less frequently than men. If you are a male, you are probably not going to change your gender, but you can work on your ability to empathize. Empathy is a key ingredient when it comes to being able to forgive - if we are able to imagine ourselves being capable of committing a similar offense, we will be more likely to forgive. If we are able to find similarities between our offenders and ourselves, we may find it easier to forgive them for what they did.

There is evidence that this works particularly well for men when they focus on their ability to commit a similar offense. If a man can imagine a situation where they commit a similar offense, they became much more able to forgive. Unfortunately it is not possible to do this with all situations, and often these are the most difficult.

To Think About:
How aware are you of the effect of a conflict on you and the affected relationships?
Have you ever sought to exact revenge upon someone who has hurt you?
If you've been hurt, can you imagine yourself doing it to someone else?

God and Consequences

Forgiveness motivated by:

- Belief in Karma
- The Burden of Guilt

A number of studies found that if a person believes in the existence of God, they are more likely to engage in forgiveness.[19] The study didn't specify which god they believed in, only that you believe there is a god out there, and he's keeping score. These people find it easier to forgive for one of two reasons:

Guilt

People who have a belief in a higher being may feel that they should "do the right thing". Everyone's moral code is different, but if you believe in a god, he/she probably expects you to be good (at least when other people are looking).

Fear/ Karma

When people believe they will eventually be paid back for their actions by some universal score-keeping force, they are more likely to choose to be "good" (such as forgiving). Commonly held beliefs among people who believe in a god are that their actions result in consequences in their own lives reflecting on how they have treated others – a "reap what you sow" mentality.

The belief in a cosmic cause and effect results in increased empathy towards others and an ability to forgive oneself when in the wrong, as you believe that one day you'll be paid back in kind for these actions.

To Think About:
What is your moral code?
What would stop you from doing something bad that you could get away without ever being penalised?
Have you ever done something that later resulted in an equivalent consequence for you – either good or bad?

Grace and Passing The Debt On

Forgiveness motivated by:

- Experiencing forgiveness first
- God's justice
- Community pressure
- Prayer

> "Throughout life people will make you mad, disrespect you and treat you bad. Let God deal with the things they do, 'cause hate in your heart will consume you too." - Will Smith

According to the previously mentioned research if a person regularly goes to church they are more likely to forgive than if they don't. It appears that the beliefs of churchgoers tend more towards forgiving than those who don't attend. Why do Christians forgive more than your average Joe? The study found that the Christian faith is correlated to the ability to forgive, as distinct from those who believe in a god. There are a number of factors that cause Christians to lean more frequently towards forgiveness:

Grace and Forgiveness

For a Christian, the consequences for the wrong things they've done are forgiven when Jesus died on the cross. The concept of forgiveness is foundational to the Christian faith. As a result, they are expected to forgive others in turn:

> "For if you forgive other people when they sin against you, your heavenly Father will also forgive you. But if you do not forgive others their sins, your Father will not forgive your sins." [20]   - Jesus

Christians believe their God is perfectly just and one day will judge the world and Jesus satisfies the need for this perfect justice when he dies instead of them. A Christian forgives a debt knowing that one day there is an accounting for debts in a highest courtroom. In a sense, they are almost passing the debt on. It's a similar concept to the way a company writes off a debt. They will write off the debt as bad, but the debt may still be paid in litigation down the line. If you don't believe there is a higher court to turn to, it's entirely up to you to get the debt paid. Getting sufficient payment on an emotional debt is far from common, leaving you with a debt that may not ever be paid.

Forgiving the Unforgiveable

There are similarities between forgiving in this way, and the twelve-step program used by Alcoholics and similar groups. Members admit that they are powerless over alcohol and need help from a "higher power"; seeking guidance and strength through prayer and meditation from God or a Higher Power of their own understanding. As part of this, they take a moral inventory of all the resentments they have towards people. Sometimes forgiving seems impossible. This is where the twelve-step approach might work. If you can't do it on your own, ask the help of a higher power. In the same way, we may need to ask the help of a higher power to forgive the unforgiveable.

Sometimes a debt may be so huge that we feel like we could never let them off without some form of compensation. For many, believing in a God who will ensure payment is made in the future, helps them to forgive in the present – it isn't about just cancelling a debt never to see it repaid; it's about passing the case on to a higher court. In the same way that legal systems allow for an appeal to a higher court, these people take their appeals to a court higher in power than the one in their own hearts, believing their god will one day make everything right.

I recently watched a YouTube video of the court case of the Green River killer, Gary Ridgway. He was convicted of murdering 49 women, but confessed to nearly twice that number. A number of family members of the victims addressed Ridgeway directly, most justifiably condemning him to die a painful death, to rot in hell, calling him an animal among other things. Ridgway sat there emotionless and unmoving until Robert Rule, father of Linda Rule, got up to speak,

"Mr. Ridgway, um, there are people here who hate you. I'm not one of them. You've made it difficult to live up to what I believe, and what God says to do, and that is forgive, and he doesn't say to forgive just certain people, he says forgive all. So you are forgiven."

Ridgway was moved to tears by his words, in a way that all the harsh condemnations couldn't. When you need to forgive the unforgiveable, remembering Robert Rule's example might help.

Community
The closeness of community in many churches that Christians attend means there is an incentive to work through an issue, rather than walking away. A rift can affect the whole community, giving leaders within a church, incentive to get involved and broker a solution between parties involved. This doesn't always lead to forgiveness, but can help and definitely pave the path.

When All Else Fails, Pray?

A recent study done in the U.S., revealed the way in which prayer may affect the brains of people[21]. The researchers scanned the brains of Franciscan nuns, Buddhists, Sikhs and Sufis -- along with everyday people new to meditation from many different types of faith. What they found was fascinating, and may help us to improve at empathizing with others. Using brain-imaging techniques, the study found that spiritual practices like prayer, meditation and breathing techniques can alter the neural connections of the brain, and result in "long-lasting states of unity, peacefulness and love." These neural networks often develop within a matter of weeks, rather than years. They also found that a strong belief in God multiplies the effect on the brain and increases "social awareness and empathy while subduing destructive feelings and emotions."

Although prayer or meditation is not essential to successfully forgiving, it may be beneficial in building your ability to empathize if you do try to wish good towards them by praying for their good.

To Think About:
Do you think it'd be easier or harder for you to forgive if you thought God was going to do the judging for you at some point down the track?
Would a close-knit community make it easier or harder to forgive, do you think?

Empathy Vs Narcissism

If you haven't realized yet, empathy plays a key role in being able to permanently forgive. Most people are usually able to foster some level of empathy towards others at least some of the time. Yet there is a certain type of person who will rarely, if ever, demonstrate this ability. They are commonly referred to as narcissists. If you are one, you're going to find it very difficult to forgive others, and they can sometimes make life very difficult.

The "entitled narcissist" [22] is highlighted by researchers in one study as a group of people who have a well-defined sense of being "owed" by the world. They are more reluctant to forgive someone without receiving a form of repayment, and they will likely insist on extra conditions being added. They overestimate potential costs of forgiving and are overly sceptical of any potential benefits. Narcissists are extremely bad at empathizing, which is a key ingredient in forgiveness. A narcissist will be less forgiving even with relatively minor issues due to having a skewed sense of entitlement and an inflated concept of interpersonal debts.

By definition, an entitled person is preoccupied with defending their rights and collecting the debts they're owed. They will protect themselves from being hurt a second time, and may go about claiming repayment of debts in a way that is cold and calculating. They can be easily offended by others, and are often reluctant to "lose face" by forgiving.

I Can't/Don't Want to Forgive

I Don't Want to Forgive Them

You're quite happily harbouring a grudge. You don't want to forgive them, nor will you ever. Yet you are aware that the grudges you are carrying are affecting your life and relationships. In my experience, if a person REALLY wants lasting freedom, genuine forgiveness is the fastest and best way to get it. If someone doesn't want to do it, no-one can make them, but they are going to lose out somewhere.

I've Never Forgiven Before

Some people may be quite unfamiliar with the whole concept of forgiveness. It's possible that their family background was quite tough and forgiveness was seen as a weakness, while revenge was perceived as type of strength, and usually the safest option. It may have been that their parents and role models were hard taskmasters, having high expectations and being quick to judge and criticise. If you've never seen forgiveness lived out before or experienced it personally, this may be a new concept.

I Got Revenge and Now It's Out of Control!

When we find ourselves in a situation of escalating tit-for-tat, it can be quite complex to bring it to an end - reconciliation and forgiveness is going to be tricky. Both sides will have a story of why they are right. How on earth do we forgive someone who keeps on hurting us? It's easy when it's in the past, but when they're right up in our face, and they're saying and doing nasty things to us every day, how do we bring it to a close? We look at reconciliation and how to make peace in Part 2.

I Would Never Do What They Did.

It is possible that we can't imagine ever acting in a similar way as the person who hurt us, regardless of the possible mitigating circumstances. If we can't conceive a situation where we would act in the same way, we may find that we are less able to empathise and forgive. If we can remember or imagine a time when we did the same thing, we may possibly find it easier to forgive someone else[23]. This is limited though, as there are certain acts that many of us simply can't imagine doing.

Some research actually suggests that if we believe ourselves incapable of committing an offense, we might actually end up blowing it out of proportion (e.g.: "I would NEVER do that").

I Can't Specifically Identify What I Need to Forgive

A person may know there's something they have to deal with. They know they're carrying an emotional burden that's weighing them down, but they just can't put their finger on it. They may have had it a lot of their life, and sometimes they're almost aware of it, but it seems to float in their peripheral vision, just out of reach.

Often the place to start is by asking what we were owed by the person.

Perhaps we've tried forgiving someone a million times, but just can't seem to do it. We've been to counselling and talked about it *ad nauseum*, but still can't completely shut it down. The heart is a funny thing, in love as well as hate; it rarely does what it's told. Just simply saying, "I forgive" isn't enough for the heart to fall into line. Sometimes it's a short process, sometimes a longer one. The important thing is to not give up and keep focused. In the next chapter, we look at how the heart doesn't always do what the head may tell it to. Perhaps you've tried everything else. You've got nothing to lose.

Chapter 3 Exercises

1. What standard do you use to measure your own self-worth? What do you use to measure the worth of others?

2. Which part of forgiving do you find the hardest? E.g.: you don't want to do it, can't do it, the forgiveness doesn't last?

Journal Exercise:

You will revisit this following exercise relationship frequently for the many of the coming Chapter Exercises so choose one you're happy to work on regularly. Ideally, it needs to be someone close to you who hurt you deeply on more than one occasion. Don't choose one that is too traumatic for you to handle (e.g.: exes, close friends etc.) or too far in the past that you don't remember. Write as if no one else will read it, so protect it accordingly (i.e. don't give it away). Answer with total honesty.

Once you've chosen the person, write at length about the occasions that they hurt you. Pay particular attention to where you feel most emotional, and ask why. For each occasion, record the following:

Situation
2. What was the background?

3. How much did you trust the relationship then? How much now? What changed?

4. Explain blow-by-blow in detail, what they did to you?

5. What should they have done instead in this situation? What did you expect from them? E.g.: received Betrayal/ owed Loyalty, received Apathy/ owed Love, etc.

Action
6. How did you respond? Did you retaliate, confront, ignore, involve a third party etc.

7. Did your actions make things worse or better?

Result
8. Is the relationship different from before it happened - think in terms of positive and negative feelings towards them?

9. Is the relationship different from before?

10. Do you still feel angry towards them? Do you want revenge?

11. Imagine a circumstance where the other person could put things right. Anything is possible. What would need to happen? What are the chances of this happening?

Reflection
12. As you wrote, did you excuse them, justify or condone their actions in any way?

13. When do you last recall seeking revenge on someone? Did it feel right or wrong?

Flip It
Use the same method to write from the perspective of the person who hurt you without your biases. Write as if you were them.

Chapter 4: Heart vs. Head

Just saying, "I forgive you" doesn't work. Forgiveness must be "heartfelt".

Imagine you're watching the famous Shakespearean play, Romeo and Juliet. The lights dim, you sit back in your seat expecting to see one of the most famous plays of all time. But what you get is slightly different.

"O Romeo, Romeo! Wherefore art thou Romeo? Deny thy father and refuse thy name. Or if thou wilt not, be but sworn my love and I'll no longer be a Capulet." Juliet whispers breathlessly

To which Romeo sensitively replies, "Sorry Jules, our relationship just doesn't make logical sense. You're pretty hot, but your family is a deal breaker, what with them and us being archenemies and all. Let's just be friends."

Err, hang on, that doesn't sound right... In the actual play, Romeo pledges his undying love, whatever the cost, however foolish, and that's the story. Without that, the story would be dull.

If Romeo and Juliet's hearts defer to common sense it wouldn't reflect the reality of being in love. The struggle between the heart and head is common fare for storytellers in the literary, dramatic and musical spheres. There's nothing as fascinating as watching a person overcome long odds to reach the desires of their heart.

Just like Romeo's heart, ours too has a will of its own. Understanding human emotions has been put in the "too hard" basket by some in the scientific and research communities. However understanding the "why" behind our actions is important if we are to try and alter our behaviour and forgive, trust and love once again.

The question that really stumps many people is: How do we make our hearts listen to our heads?

Your Heart is in the Driver's Seat

"Educating the mind without educating the heart is no education at all"

- Aristotle

There is a difference between the heart and the head. Many believe that the mind makes the decisions, and our hearts follow. We see examples of people proving this wrong all the time by making bad decisions based on their feelings or emotions, and not using obvious logic and reason - the man who cheats on the wife he loves, the investor who bets it all on a feeling, or the voter who chooses the best looking politician. All have one thing in common: reason is not the core of their decision-making.

Any reference made to the heart here is not an attempt to reinvent many years of psychological theory. There are many competing theories on what is commonly referred to as the "subconscious", no one of which is predominant. "The heart" is only a metaphor to describe the part of us that it is not subservient to the control of our minds (i.e. the will).

For the purpose of our definition, the "heart" does the following: It does not always act in accordance with the directions from our minds or the use of logic, wisdom, or common sense; it may remember things that our conscious minds have repressed, that we need to dig up to deal with.

Marketers have known that the heart and the head are separate for the best part of a century. John B Watson pioneered the application of psychology in advertising. He believed that in order for advertising to be effective, it should appeal to three innate emotions: love, fear and rage.[24] Watson was the first person to sell toothpaste using this technique - not because of the dental hygiene benefits, but because whiter teeth give you more sex appeal. He recognised that to sell a car you need to appeal to people's emotions first, common sense second. How many car ads have you seen that imply that you will be more attractive, popular, and fun if you buy a certain car? They will, however mention the features, the great value for money, and the warranty to close the deal.

First show how it will help a person reach their aspirations, then let them justify what their heart desires with the features. Advertisers have known for decades what the rest of us don't.

We make decisions with our hearts, and our heads follow along behind, trying to justify and claim credit for our actions, and restore order to the trail of carnage our hearts have left in their wake. Advertising is ultimately about getting people to make a decision.

How many times have you or a friend fallen in love with someone who was bad for you? At the time you were probably blinded by their features - the strong physical attraction you felt towards them (perhaps a benefit or two also), but couldn't recognize the many drawbacks or costs at the time.

A Heartfelt Apology

People often believe that their heads can tell their hearts that they've forgiven something, and to an extent this is true where a person is highly disciplined. Until we have forgiven with our heart, we won't entirely be free of it. Often times, when we haven't forgiven it is because our hearts are clinging to a desire to be repaid, so we seek revenge in little, often barely noticeable ways. In one research study[25], clinging to an internal desire for revenge while we are releasing our anger externally had very limited success in reducing anger and experiencing greater freedom. If anger remains not dealt with for a while, it can make us sick - in our hearts, minds and bodies.

When we talk about a "heartfelt apology", we are inadvertently distinguishing between the offer of a genuine apology (from the heart), and one that isn't fully meant (from the head). The process of "falling in forgiveness" requires full commitment from our hearts.

It's What They Owe You That Matters

Kim's boyfriend, Jeff, decided to break up with her one day, without any prior warning or explanation. It took her completely by surprise, as they'd had some of their best dates together near the end. She was working night shifts, and working through the death of a close friend - both highly stressful things to deal with on their own.

As Jeff was driving Kim home one night, he drops the bombshell that it's over. He said he couldn't stay and chat because he had a game of pickup football in the park. Kim didn't react well, taking the opportunity to tell him exactly what she thought of him. Jeff completely cuts contact with her and avoids her over the following months. Kim is feeling depressed but knows she needs to forgive him, and tries to every single day.

Kim feels that Jeff owed her time to prepare by expressing that he wasn't happy. Instead she was blindsided at a time when she was at her weakest. When Kim realizes that she has merely been forgiving with her head, not her heart, it is the beginning of the breakthrough she needs.

Emotions Are Stronger Than Logic

"The heart has its reasons of which reason knows nothing." – Blaise Pascall

My Granddad tried to quit smoking for many years without success. He failed because he didn't have the emotional motivation. He wanted to quit, but didn't have a strong enough reason to motivate him.

That was until one evening while he was having a cheeky cigarette outside a theatre. He was distracted halfway through, and to his horror he somehow found himself with the lit end of the cigarette in his mouth. That single mouthful of ash, the severely blistered tongue, and the urging of his daughter was enough to motivate him to quit smoking forever.

It is emotion that moves us to change behaviour - our hearts give us the momentum, and logic helps us justify. For my granddad, tangible pain was what he needed. Understanding this is essential if we are to permanently leave our baggage behind. At many points we may notice that our head tries to take over during the process of forgiving. Learning to listen to our heart and letting it show us what IT needs to heal is an important, but delicate ingredient in the recipe of forgiveness.

Your Heart Has a Better Memory

"It has been said, 'time heals all wounds.' I do not agree. The wounds remain. In time, the mind, protecting its sanity, covers them with scar tissue and the pain lessens. But it is never gone." – Rose Kennedy

Even though our heads may forget, our hearts do not. We might spend years trying to bury a painful memory, often with some success, but beneath it there remains scarring and residual pain.

We may have forgotten something that happened many years before. For one reason or another, we have no recollection of things that happened to us in our childhood. It may be that our minds have limited storage capacity (mine definitely has), and often misplaces valuable information. Perhaps it could have happened when we were very young, or perhaps it was a traumatic experience that we have since blocked out to cope.

Learning to ask what we need to forgive is the first step. A lot of the time, people think they already know the solution to their problem. "I need to forgive my dad", they might say - and that may be the case, but it's possible that that's not where to start. First we need to listen to our heart. This starts by clearing our mind of any preconceived ideas we might have.

When Your Heart Gets Stuck on Repeat

Have you ever thought to yourself "life would be perfect if I just had these"?

We may sometimes wish we had a replay button for the many mistakes we've made in life, in the same way we love to replay the wrongs we have had done to us by others. We'll look at them from every angle like a slow motion replay. We'll do this for a long time after the event; we often can't stop even if we try. The best examples are usually following breakups. It is common in the proceeding weeks and months after a significantly painful event in our lives. The process is called rumination. Excessive rumination can blow facts out of proportion, inflate what we feel owed - to a point where others couldn't ever pay us back even if they wanted to.

The origin of the word rumination derives from the Latin word 'ruminare', which literally refers to the act of a cow as it chews cud. Cows have 4 stomachs. They process food at least 4 times. We process our hurts a lot more than that. In most cases the modern term describes excessive worrying, or, according to the dictionary[26]: "obsessive or abnormal reflection upon an idea or deliberation over a choice." More specifically, rumination is a coping strategy characterized by a passive and repetitive focus on the negative and damaging features of a stressful transaction. It's common when we've been hurt to do this, but it is rarely helpful. Excessive rumination prolongs and exacerbates our unforgiving nature, which results in a downward spiral of negative emotions.

Other Fish in the Sea

The old adage "there are other fish in the sea" offered by helpful friends to those recently heartbroken, is to distract them from ruminating and keep their situation and the facts in perspective. Staying busy, getting active, doing new things are all helpful in preventing ourselves to mope around and dwell on the situation for too long.

The strategy of increasing activity for a time after an event can override self-pity, and allow us to reduce the significance of specific details to promote forgiveness. By putting the painful details out of our mind for a time, we create a sense of distance to get some perspective and clarity. A level of discipline is required to successfully pull this off when all we want to do is sit and be still when we are in pain.

Reducing rumination is strongly related to making progress in forgiveness. If we can make a habit of it, we will be better at forgiving. The more people ruminate, the more they desire vengeance on the person who hurt them. The results concluded that minimising rumination would speed up the forgiveness process.

How Do I Recall Past Hurts Without Ruminating?

Allowing ourselves to recall painful memories is important to the healing process, but we must understand the difference between rumination and constructive reflection. If we don't we'll end up plunging back into rumination, vengeful thoughts and unforgiving. Having a process in place before we re-enter painful memories will allow us to have entry and exit points to avoid the rumination spiral.

I once spent the day damming up a river with people from a mountain tribe in Thailand. We couldn't stop the flow of it, even with the many huge rocks we dropped in to block it up. The best we could do was slow it, and divert the flow. I was determined to make the river stop, so I jammed up every gap in one of the dams, and kept building the rock wall higher and wider. However high I built it, the river would just flow up further onto the banks around. It's impossible to "stop" ruminating; it just flows around whatever we try to stop it with. We can't stop thoughts, but we can divert them toward areas that are more constructive, changing the way they flow.

When a company wants to copy a competitor's product, they start with a finished product and reverse engineer it by working backwards. When we find ourselves thinking vengeful thoughts (for me, it's usually when my thoughts get vengeful), I stop and retrace the steps I took to get there. Identifying the thing that triggered this thought lets me divert my thoughts next time it happens, similar to the way we divert a river.

Your Head Says Yes, Your Heart Says No

Many people think that all they need to do to forgive is say, "I forgive you" and be done with it - nothing more required. This may work for some things, but for the big stuff, there's a lot more they'll need to do.

In many Western countries where we can spend 20+ years in formal education, we might easily come to the conclusion that our heads make all the big decisions. For someone with this background, they may think that saying "I forgive you", is all it will take. Some of the most highly educated people I know (and love) are the least aware or interested in what is going on in their hearts. This is a common delusion prevalent amongst many of us. When these same people get hurt, they have little idea what to do, or how to fix it, except ignore it or numb the pain away. It may take something like bad health or another issue outside of their control for them to really stop and take the time to listen to their hearts.

Perhaps you are one of these people. Perhaps you are reading this book because you have experienced something that is slowing you down, or has stopped you in your tracks. You don't know why it's happened, or how come there isn't some sort of magical, quick fix solution you can take that will permanently fix it. Even if you could put your finger on what the exact problem was in the first place, the first place to start is to find exactly what our hearts feel owed - what the person who hurt you SHOULD have done, rather than what they DID.

Chapter 4 Exercises

In your notebook, using the same relationship as previously in the Chapter 3 Exercises, think of as many negative encounters with this person as you can remember. Write a paragraph or more in your notebook. Think of 5 if you can. A few questions to answer:

1. What happened? Who, what, when, where, why, other people, and issues that were involved.

2. How was it resolved?

3. What should they have done to you instead?

4. How did you feel about it? How do you feel now?

5. How long ago did it happen? Did it alter the way you relate to each other?

6. Do you want to forgive this person now? What would it take for you to forgive them with your whole heart?

7. How committed and/or invested are you in this relationship currently?

8. If you could get revenge in any way, what revenge would result in full repayment of the debt?

9. Do you feel that the benefits of letting go of the hurts outweigh the costs that you have sustained? Refer to "benefits of forgiveness".

10. Review each thing that this person did to you, have you ever done this to others?

11. Can you imagine a situation, however extreme, where you did?

Section 2: How To Forgive

Chapter 5: The Debt

Our hearts chase unpaid debts long after our brains have given up.

Motorhome resident Dennis Quigly woke up at 1am feeling the familiar tickle that told him his old bladder needed to be emptied. While in the toilet, he heard a peculiar noise under his motorhome that sounded a lot like a person, so he phoned the police. When the police arrived, they found a garden hose hanging from the sewage tank, left by someone who had sucked on the end to create a siphon to draw out the contents of the tank. "Apparently, the suspect was attempting to steal gasoline and got the sewage tank instead," said Officer Tom Umporowicz.

When Umporowicz arrived, he also noted a large quantity of untreated sewage on the ground left by the culprit, who had thrown up what he had ingested. The officer followed the trail to a nearby car and found a teenage boy curled up and retching. The boy asked the officer to call the medics. The boy was not arrested as Quigly declined to file a complaint, figuring the boy had been punished enough. "It's the best laugh I've ever had," Quigly told police. [27]

Debt Collection Agencies and Forgiveness

The young would-be petrol thief had an expectation of what he was receiving. What he got instead was very different, and left him with a bad taste in his mouth. We all expect things from certain types of relationships, when we fail to receive what we expect; it leaves us with a bad taste in our mouths.

Parents and romantic partners are often the relationships that most of us have the highest expectations of. When these aren't met, we feel let down. We are guaranteed to be let down by someone at some point. This creates a debt that often can't ever completely be repaid, even when revenge is carried out in full. One way to define forgiveness is the cancellation of a debt by a person who has been hurt or wronged. The concept of relational debt has been around a long time before 'Forgiveness Research' came on the scene.

Forgive Us Our Debts

"And forgive us our debts, as we also have forgiven our debtors" – Jesus

People will commonly use the phrase "they owe me an apology" when they've been hurt. It rolls off the tongue easily, but why would a person who hurt them owe them something? And what is it that makes an apology so important anyway?

Every heart has an innate, inbuilt sense of justice. Even the most twisted of people have some sort of "code" they abide by, it just may seem wrong to everyone else. When the heart recognises that there is a transaction still owing, it will harass us for payment until it gets what it is after. I think of it a bit like a mini debt-collection agency - our heart will use any means possible until the debt is fully paid – in the meantime, we might not get a lot of sleep, feel stressed, get sick (hence the phrase "heartsick"), anxious or depressed.

We need to begin to think about our relational hurts as a debt that one person owes another. One study [28] defined them as "a betrayal of the way we expect to be treated (obligations), which in the process creates a "moral debt".

"That's Not Fair"

"Justice has nothing to do with what goes on in a courtroom; Justice is what comes out of a courtroom" - Clarence Darrow

If, like me, you grew up with brothers or sisters, you can probably remember a situation where they were treated better than you. You may have cried out to your parents "That's not fair" – most children have a pretty strong sense of fairness.

We have a desire for equality and fairness built into our DNA. When we don't receive what's fair, we get angry. This same principle is at the very heart of forgiveness. When we are unfairly treated or hurt, it usually isn't what we deserve and so something needs to be done to make it right again.

Long after our minds have moved on from the pain (and sometimes the memory) of being hurt, our hearts acquire the debt and continue to chase payment. Unfortunately, a lot of us aren't very good at listening to our hearts; so we tend to either ignore it or just learn to live with the constant harassment our hearts give us. The issue for most of us is that we don't know how to clear the books – to cancel those longstanding debts that are still hanging around.

When It Costs More Than It's Worth

Have you ever thought about how we value our relationships? Why do we stay friends with certain people, and let others go? Everyone has different ways of prioritizing relationships, but at some point, most of us look at how beneficial the relationship is to us over how much it costs us in an effort to maintain it.

Social Exchange Theory looks at this cost-benefit model of relationships. Its primary assumption is that benefits must outweigh costs, or a person will discard the relationship.

Benefits can include companionship, acceptance and support etc. Costs can involve time, money, effort, relational pain and other factors as such.

Outcome = Benefits – Costs

Costs = time, money, effort, pain etc.

Benefits = companionship, acceptance, support, association, etc.

When someone hurts us, there is a cost (experiencing emotional pain) to maintaining this relationship. We may relive it every time we see them. The larger the hurt, the stronger the pain, and hence, the cost, and therefore the more likely we are to sever the relationship; even if we recognise there are significant benefits to us (as in some cases of marital unfaithfulness).

A number of Forgiveness research studies[29] recognise forgiveness as a "cost reduction" strategy, that in forgiving a past hurt, we are actually reducing the costs involved, and so we are more likely to retain the relationship. One study hypothesized that "repayment facilitates forgiveness by reducing the size of the debt, or 'injustice gap'"[30]

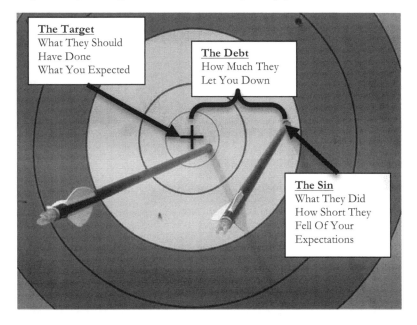

The Injustice Gap

In determining the size of the gap we need to forgive, we need to find reference points to establish where the gap begins and where it ends. A forgiveness gap begins when what we feel we are entitled to, doesn't happen. We can get hurt when the standard we set isn't met – when the mark is missed.

Missing the Mark

Archery has provided a reliable illustration of how this works. Archery competitions in the middle ages required competitors to fire arrows at a far away target, such as a replica stag or bull made of iron, specifically at the heart, now commonly referred to as the "bull's-eye". The archers were firing long distances and therefore, adjudicators were required to inspect the target to see if they hit the mark. If the arrow missed the mark, they would wave a flag and cry out "sin".

The word sin derives from Old English "synn", recorded in use as early as the 9th century. The same root word appears in several other Germanic languages such as Old Norse (synd), or German (Sünde). Of course, we all associate the word "sin" with a very different meaning, of judgement, of condemnation, and wrongdoing. Originally though, the word meant "to miss the mark" or "to miss the target".

Defining the Mark

Reference points can be quite useful in life. Athletes have personal best times, closely following their competitors to see how successful they are, sailors used the stars, artists use landmarks, and managers set goals. When it comes to working out what debts, if any, need repaying, there are two questions we must start with.

1: "What should have happened?" or "What should they have done?"
2: "How far did it miss by?" "What did they do instead?"

As a boy, I regularly did archery. I used to love pretending that I'd have a spasm, and fire an arrow up in the air, just to see how far it would go, just like archers in those medieval war movies. It was well worth the long walk to retrieve the arrow to find out.
The injustice gap is the distance between what should have happened (the mark) and what we got instead. It may be a near miss or we might have shot someone in the next suburb, but quantifying this distance allows us to have a rough measurement of what needs to be forgiven. A "sin" is when we miss the mark. The "debt" is measuring how much it was missed by.

Forgiving Betrayal

John kept trying to forgive his wife, Jackie. They were going through a difficult marriage counselling process after they separated. Jackie did many small things, including putting him down, slandering him to friends, even family and their children. She constantly criticized. He could never do enough to please her. He knew he was angry with her for something, but couldn't really put his finger on it. What did Jackie actually do to him? It was never one single big thing, always small things which he could have handled if it wasn't so constant.

But when asked what she failed to do, well, John knew exactly what was missing. Loyalty, love, support. The trick was all in how the question was framed. When they both were able to do that, they were able to then pull their marriage back together. John and Jackie subsequently had a number of very happy years together.

Foundational Principles

It Doesn't Matter If They Aren't Sorry

It stands to reason that a person is more likely to forgive certain things when they get a "heartfelt apology". But even if someone doesn't do this, it's never impossible. Studies show that [31] if one party isn't truly sorry for what they did, it doesn't necessarily prevent the other from forgiving, although it does make it harder.

In the same way a company writes off a bad debt, we should be able to write off the bad debts in our lives independently of any involvement of the debtor. They cannot hold us captive if we choose not to let them. To truly let go of our baggage, we don't need their permission, or involvement. Even if we do force an apology out of them, it's not the end of the world if they don't mean it. The power to forgive is always ours – and it can't be taken from us unless we allow it.

Debts Don't Affect Anyone But You

Quite often a debt doesn't affect anyone but the person who's been hurt, so it's not essential to take anyone else into consideration. It doesn't matter where the other person is, or if there still exists a close relationship with them. This means that we aren't considering anyone else's feelings or needs. It doesn't matter if the other person knows they have hurt us, it is about satisfying what our heart desires, so that justice can be served. It doesn't even matter if the person has disappeared, or is dead - the process of forgiving debts is still just as possible and as effective.

Don't Try To Excuse the Debt

"It is better to offer no excuse than a bad one."   — George Washington

It's common and natural to make excuses for people who we are close to, and/or love, when they hurt us. Especially when we know their history and baggage, we may find ourselves justifying unacceptable behaviour with "it's not their fault", because someone else wounded them first.

In making excuses for someone, our head is inadvertently robbing our heart of the justice it is chasing. Everyone has had bad things done to them, nevertheless, we can't let this distract us from the fact that the actions of the people we love need to be fully accounted for if we are to let them off.

There is a very good reason we are fully apportioning responsibility even to people whom we love and care for. For a debt to be fully written off, we have to have a full accounting. If we try to excuse their actions, it will prevent this from happening. It's not about anything other than paying the debt our heart feels owed. We don't need to be embarrassed if we don't think it's relevant – it still matters.

> *No Discounts*
>
> *Joe fought constantly with his father Frank as he was growing up. Frank was a stable provider and good to his mother. It was the things that Frank said and did that left Joe with some serious baggage.*
>
> *Joe's childhood experience of Frank growing up was that he was mostly absent emotionally. He regularly hurt Joe both physically and verbally - beating him, evicting him from the house, saying he was unlovable and unwanted.*
>
> *Frank though, had first learned these habits from his dad. Frank had received the same treatment from his parents, only much worse. His father then took him in, only to abuse and reject him again later on.*
>
> *It was natural for Joe to justify his dad's shortcomings out of the love he felt for him. He could have easily explained them away due to the tough hand Frank had been dealt. Joe realised though, that in doing so he was short-changing his heart of the necessary justice it required. When Joe recognised that his heart needed the debt to be fully accounted for, the peace and freedom came in quick order.*

Debts Need to Be SPECIFIC!!!

"Let me explain something to you: my husband once offended me on July 6th 1978. I can tell you exactly where I was sitting, and what he was eating. Most people have a memory of important dates and times. Now if somebody gave me/loaned me $5000. I would remember SOME of the circumstances surrounding it - because you, sir, seem to have a very, very good memory of everything you did - calling the bank, calling the title company, getting the checks, sitting down and going over everything - the only thing you don't have a memory of is "Can I borrow $5000?." Judgment to the plaintiff for the amount of $5000 - thank you." - Judge Judy

I have a secret obsession. I watch Judge Judy. No BS, she calls it as she sees it. She's often quite sympathetic, but one thing she can't stand is someone who isn't specific about the details of their case (she often judges in favour of the person who has the best grasp of the specifics of the case, as they're usually the ones with nothing to hide).

When it comes to accounting for our own debts, we need to apply the same demanding standards that Judge Judy does to her cases. It's not enough to say, "I forgive you". We have to identify exactly where the gaps of injustice exist.

How to Recognise Debts: Red Flags

Vague feelings don't cut it for Judge Judy, and they shouldn't for us either. We can't just have a vague feeling that we are owed something. It's often obvious when we've been hurt, but the specific "debt" may be a lot less forthcoming. We can start by finding the mark, how exactly it was missed, and by how much? For every missed mark, there may be multiple "debts" that need to be forgiven. Often, the bigger the hurt, the more debts that need to be cancelled. In the next chapter, we'll learn simple steps on how to do this.

The most foolproof way to know what to focus on forgiving is by noticing when negative emotions pop up. We can use them like red flags to recognize where a debt is still owed. The three big ones are:

Anger   Do we get angry when we recall a memory - perhaps replaying ways we get even through violence or other means? If so, there's probably something there we need to forgive. Sometimes the way we replay a memory will tell us about what we feel owed also.

Fear   Do we feel a sense of fear grip us when we are reminded of a particular situation or memory? What is it that we are afraid of?

Sadness   Why do we get afraid or depressed because of a certain situation? What exactly are we sad about? What could be there that we need to forgive? If a relationship has ended or been altered dramatically, your sadness/depression may be as a result of this.

Big Debts

The size of the debt is reliant on two factors: how close they were to us and what they did. A deep hurt will require time and multiple layers of forgiveness before we see noticeable changes.

1: The Relationship

The closer the relationship, the more trust is involved, and the more that we're owed. When someone we trust hurts us, it will create a much bigger debt than if a stranger did the same thing. The more we let someone into our life, the more they can hurt us when they fail to meet our expectations. If a complete stranger on the street verbally abuses you, it'll be easy to brush it off. On the other hand, if your best friend does the same, it will hurt deeply. This is why family members often grate against one another so easily. Due to the trust and proximity between families, even tiny things can end in grudge matches that last a lifetime.

A Knife In The Back

Regina took Jessie under her wing she helped her pull her life together by mentoring her and giving her life advice when she needed it. Regina was closer to Jessie than a big sister and knew all of her deepest secrets, fears and hopes.

When Regina moved states, Jessie organised her farewell party, as she was really good at party planning. Everything was going perfectly at the party until Regina took it upon herself to publically slander Jessie in front of all their mutual friends during her farewell speech. She categorically denounced every aspect of Jessie's character, concluding that Jessie was simply a bad person with no redeeming features. She even tried to justify her by saying it would "benefit" her in the long term.

Jessie was devastated for years. A few years later, Regina came back into town to get married. Although she never apologized, Regina asked Jessie to organise her hen party as she was hoping for a chance to reconcile, but Regina didn't speak to her or thank her afterwards, and didn't ever contact her again. Jessie later found out that she stayed in touch with and visited mutual friends, but not her.

An average friend wouldn't have got to Jessie like this, but the way Regina systematically took apart Jessie's character means she still struggles to trust older women who befriend her.

One of the clearest examples that I have seen of family members hurting each other is when one family member sexually abuses another. One study described it as follows: "a trusted person, who was supposed to love and protect the survivor, has instead manipulated her through lies and misrepresentations about moral standards"[32]. When a person is sexually abused, they are owed a debt of unconditional love and fierce protection by their family members, but instead they receive lies, manipulation, and a great deal of abuse. Very few debts will be larger than this. Incest survivors face higher rates of psychological health problems such as depression, anxiety, low self-esteem, marital difficulties, suicidal thoughts, self-blame, guilt, eating disorders, substance abuse. They also experience interpersonal issues rife with conflict, poor social adjustment, feelings of isolation, and impaired judgement about the trustworthiness of others.[33] This doesn't mean they are beyond hope of a full recovery and a life lived to the full.

Trust = Future Expected Benefits
- Risk from Being Vulnerable

When we expect future benefits from a relationship, we are more likely to forgive as we believe it will lead to greater well-being. Individuals who find it hard to trust due to previous betrayal will stringently evaluate every interaction to determine if future outcomes will be positive.

Many have found that closeness and relationship commitment is a key predictor of the likelihood of forgiveness. Quite a few studies have looked at interpersonal trust, one defining it as: *the positive expectation that "they can count on a partner to care for them and be responsive to their needs, both now and in the future"*[34].

Proximity Is a Factor

Essentially it all comes down to trust. In forgiveness, all relationships, however tenuous, contain an element of trust that has been breached. It may be as simple as assuming it was safe to live in the same society as someone, but that is enough. Mostly though, the closer the relationship, the more trust is invested. When we're asking, "Who do I need to forgive?" another way of asking is "Who has let me down?" i.e. people of whom we expected something from, which wasn't forthcoming.

Perhaps a total stranger hurt us. Events such as rape or murder of a loved one will negatively impact our lives profoundly. Although there is little trust between the perpetrators and us, they still let us down in very basic ways. It is also worth noting that it is often harder to empathize with these people as they are total strangers and hold little significance for us.

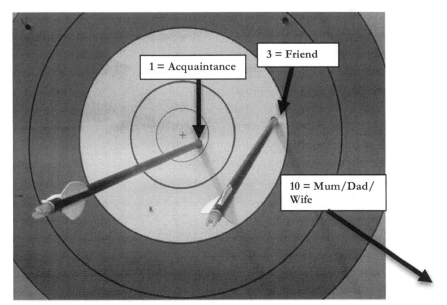

2: The Act

The most damaging wounds are usually when someone close to us does something really hurtful. Imagine there's a scale, with 10 being things like sexual abuse, violence and other deep wounds by parents and people we trust. Down the other end are little things done to us by strangers, which we register as a 1.

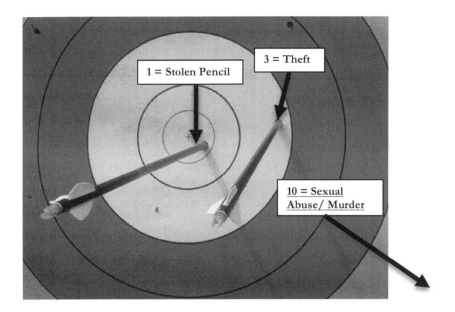

Other Elements of Big Debts

Time

"Time heals all wounds" is a common saying, and to some extent, it is true[35]. A more accurate version would be, "time allows us to get to a place where we are ready to heal", but some wounds require more than just time, and some of us may be pretty time-poor anyway.

There is usually a grieving process that needs to take place before we are ready to work through our pain, but if we can start to forgive straight away (even if our heart is not in it), forgiveness can happen sooner. If forgiveness doesn't happen and we let the wound fester we may find that it quickly becomes septic, turning into bitterness, envy, or malice - bad traits for any human being. Forgiveness is the best way of bandaging a wound to let it heal, keeping infection at bay so that it doesn't fester.

How long it takes depends entirely on us. Some people are fast forgivers; others can take long periods of time. We shouldn't beat ourselves up if we take a while sorting through our issues, though everyone is different.

Multiple Layers

With emotional pain, there is usually an underlying issue that is causing us a lot of the problems, but it may not be what we think it is. When you get a large pimple on your face, you can put concealer on it all you want, but the issue won't begin to dissipate until the skin pore is unblocked. We may feel certain that one particular issue is causing the problem, but it may be something else we have long forgotten about. Once this is removed, the symptoms can be rectified much faster.

An emotional wound that is reopened can quickly become infected. Re-infected wounds sometimes cause scar tissue - often there are layers of hurt that we need to address. For deep wounds (and big debts), it is common to find that there is a containment area around the memory to prevent psychological toxicity, to wall it off so we function in our daily lives without having to deal with the pain until we're ready. Some things hurt so much that the only way we can survive is to ignore it. Psychology refers to this as "repressed memory" – where a significant memory of a traumatic nature is no longer available to be recalled, also sometimes called "motivated forgetting"[36].

It may not be safe to take down a wall when you recognize it, so feel free to leave it up until you feel ready. Taking a wall down may unblock a tsunami of feelings that we're not ready for yet. Best to leave it up until we know we are in a place where we are ready to deal with it safely.

Trust Issues

Jason has trust issues. His last three girlfriends have dumped him because of it. He couldn't help but suspect that they were seeing other people behind his back. He had no evidence, but he couldn't stop the frequent bouts of insecurity and paranoia. In the heat of an argument, Jason accused his most recent girlfriend of cheating on him. He demanded to check her phone and emails. She dumped him, telling him he had issues. Jason had to agree.

After doing some major soul searching, he found that it all started with his first girlfriend in early high school. He was smitten with her, but she ended up leaving him for another guy in his class, going behind his back for a month before telling him.

Chipping Away

We don't always have to start with a big debt. You'll probably see quicker progress chipping away bit by bit with smaller ones and work up to it. Progress can be the most encouraging and motivating thing.

Project managers break a really big project down into bite size pieces to make each step achievable. Our hearts will show us what we need to do; we just have to start forgiving today - what we can see right in front of us. We shouldn't get discouraged if it's not happening as quickly as we'd like it to - any progress is better than none. In anything where success isn't immediately evident, when we do finally see a bit of a breakthrough, we'll be encouraged, and gain momentum. This boost will feed back into our enthusiasm for the process that we are going through and it'll become easier next time.

Chapter 5 Exercises:

Answer all questions honestly - there are no wrong answers, write them in your notebook. Have it on you always.

<u>General Questions</u>

1. When was the last time you felt you were "owed" an apology? Why? What happened?

2. Can you remember a time as a child when you were treated unfairly? What happened? What should have happened?

3. When was the last time you consciously let a relationship go because it was too hard? What was the point where you decided to let it go? What were the benefits? What were the costs?

4. Have you ever fully forgiven someone who didn't ask for or want it?

Do you feel that unable to forgive without a heartfelt apology?

Do you feel the urge to make excuses or justify someone else when they hurt you or others?

<u>Table Exercise</u>

Go to Mykeyrobinson.com/downloads and download 'The Forgiveness Worksheet'. Print off the 'Forgiving Others' tab. Using the same relationship you have been looking at up until now. (Note: You can do this for other relationships and situations also – there's no limit)
Draw up a table in your notebook with six columns.
- In Column 1, write the name of the person you are forgiving. Use their actual name e.g.: instead of "Jez" or "uncle", I will use Jeremy Hamilton, or Uncle Jeremy etc.
- In column 2: list 5 (+/-) specific times where they hurt you
- In column 3: list 3 (+/-) specific things for each thing that they did in that circumstance which impacted you negatively (the wound). Be as specific as you can. For each one, they may have hurt you in multiple ways.

- In column 4: next to each specific thing that impacted you negatively, write what they should have done in the situation (the debt)?
Don't worry about column 5 and 6 until Chapter 7 "The Forgiveness Process".

1: Who Hurt Me?	2: What Happened?	3: How Did They Hurt Me?	4: What Should They Have Done

Chapter 6: Measuring the Mark – Who to Forgive

It's about knowing which debts are owed by whom

A few years ago, my mum got upset on Mother's day. She waited for her beloved children to call her, to no avail. She'd been out at dinner with some of her close friends the night before, where one of them mentioned that it was Mother's Day the next day. When none of her children called, she was upset. She called me, wondering why I hadn't called her. I could tell by the pause that she was waiting for me to say I'd forgotten to wish her a Happy Mother's Day.

My mum was upset with me, until she found out that Mother's Day was actually the following week (the next Sunday) and realized her mistake - she'd got the date wrong by a week.

My mother didn't expect everyone to wish her a happy mother's day, rather just her kids. Just like my mum, we have different expectations depending on the relationship.

Dads In The Past

We all have expectations in relationships. Understanding specifically what we expect from each relationship is essential so we can recognize exactly how we've been let down, and cancel the associated debts. We trust certain people for certain relational needs, such as parents, doctors, teachers, accountants, lawyers, babysitters, or priests. It is this trust which make a relationship, a relationship. Part of forgiving is to pinpoint exactly what it was that went lacking.

Usually, the relationships that impact us the most are those of fathers and mothers, especially when we are young children. Until recently, research[37] has almost exclusively focused on the role of mothers to the exclusion of other caregivers. In the past, fathers were marginalized to the role of breadwinner, seen mostly as an indirect caregiver. Fathers have been traditionally seen as mostly impacting an infant indirectly via the mother.

The role that fathers play in children's lives has been increasingly recognized as essential to the upbringing of children. In colonial times, the role of the father was limited to that of a disciplinarian, teacher of life skills (children would often work as apprentices with their fathers), and breadwinner. During the Industrial Revolution there was an increased separation between children and their fathers (and later, mothers) as they went off to work for the majority of the day. As a result, education (and care) of children was outsourced to schools.

More recently, the emphasis has been on the "primary caregiver" (unrelated to gender and biological relation), encompassing the many people who influence a child as they grow up, such as nannies, grandparents, etc. In a world of single parents, and outsourced childcare, children receive care from a wider variety of people than just their parents, who are often busy working. There has been a focus on the benefits that children get from a meaningful relationship with their fathers, but more on the effect of his absence than his presence. There are lots of theories that look at how a child develops into a fully functional adult, each emphasizing the importance of different factors for healthy social and emotional development. It has been suggested that children who excel in social situations had mothers who loved them and made them feel safe, and fathers who provided exciting play and interactive challenges. Fathers have been found to heavily influence and guide intellectual and social development, especially during teenage years.

Not all relationships fulfil the same needs. Ideally, healthy paternal relationships will fulfil a different set of needs than romantic relationships. I've looked at a general framework of categories to help understand the various debts that we may feel owed. It is not an exhaustive list, but it'll get you started.

Debt Categories

For each type of relationship, there are certain things we innately expect. This is particularly true for children. We are born with an expectation that adults will provide certain things for us and expectation is part of the human nature, from childhood through to adulthood. When I was young, I was trying to climb a paling fence. My feet slipped and slid all the way down the splintered wood. Hunched on the ground, I lost count of the dozens of splinters lodged in the soles of my bleeding feet. My dad was first on the scene, but I wouldn't let him go near my feet. I got him to carry me to my mum.

For each relationship, we may find that certain factors will influence what they owed us – such as the role they played in our life (for example a doctor, teacher, or policeman), their gender, and their age – a relationship with our step-mother only a few years older than us, may feel more like peer–to-peer than parent-child. As such, loyalty and trustworthiness were debts that were of a higher priority than love or protection. Another example might be an old male surgeon who negligently performed a procedure on us. We may find the debt they owe us is more in line with a healing role (often associated with maternal) than a paternal role.

Expectations

As I've listened to people talk about unmet expectations of friends and family, it became clear that we often expect certain things from certain types of relationships. The following are only guidelines. For example, parents are often primary carers, peers are often our companions, and so forth. some others are:
- Love
- Care

- Protection
- Provision
- Identity
- Healing
- Counselling
- Teaching
- Companionship
- Secrecy
- Loyalty
- Trustworthiness

Love

Related Relationships: paternal, maternal, sibling, romantic partner, trusted peers.

There are many theories out there as to what separates people from animals. Some would say we are more intelligent, more rational and more socially complex. I have a hunch that it is our ability to love. Children come out of the womb programmed to receive love, it's what they need to function. As we grow, we may learn through trial and error how best to give love, and a lot of the process of growing up and relating to others teaches us how to give and receive love. When we are inevitably hurt during this process, we take on board things that aren't true. Fear of rejection is when we are afraid that when we offer love to somebody, they will not see us as worthy of their love. When a boy finally musters the courage to tell a girl how he feels, there's a very real chance she will throw it back in his face, run away, or both. Some relationships require love, but sometimes love is much more forthcoming from one side than the other.

Perhaps you didn't feel loved growing up? Perhaps no-one actually reciprocated love back to you in a way you needed. Perhaps many people loved you as you grew up, but you didn't know how to love others because you were shy or afraid? Whatever it was, you will still need to find affirming answers to the same two questions: "Am I loveable and worth loving?" and "is the love that I give valuable?"

Care

Related Relationships: paternal, maternal, romantic partner.

Caregivers provide for the needs of a child. Female caregivers tend to be better at catering to the physical and emotional needs of children. Males in the same position can be less capable, and may show care for children in a less tender way. Types of care can include:

Attention – Showing a particular level of interest in another.
Availability/Accessibility – Relationships usually require time to grow. When a person restricts their access and availability, it can let us down.
Resources – When a person withholds necessary resources, we may feel it reflects the low value they put on the relationship.

It is not only parents who may have a "duty of care" towards us. Doctors, police, even people in positions of religious and educational authority naturally have certain things they should give us as part of their role.

Care and healing are more frequently the domain of mothers. The "maternal instinct", as it is so often referred to, may be the reason why such a high percentage of women are nurses (92.1%) and teachers (76%).[38] As a generalization, women have a more defined instinct to care for others, and without it, the world would be a far worse place. If we had parents who weren't good at giving care, showing sympathy or an interest in our life in the way we needed it, we may need to look at this further.

Counsellor/Teacher

Related Relationships: paternal, maternal.

Both parents impart information in their own different ways. More often it is mothers who fulfil the role of teacher and counsellor, so often have a greater influence in guiding and instructing children. Perhaps our mother failed to teach us vital information, or abused the power she had, using it in some way to control or manipulates us. A lot of the time, kids take information from their parents and other adults as fact, which can lead to misinformation and exploitation.

Our actual teachers throughout school are probably included here. When I was three, I had a pre-school teacher who bit me after I bit another boy in the sandpit. I still remember her teeth marks in my arm. For the rest of school, I mistrusted teachers, and went to school reluctantly. At least I haven't bitten anyone since (in anger, at least). Perhaps we grew up with manipulative or controlling parents who withheld care as blackmail to get us to act the way that they wanted – perhaps justifying this by thinking they knew what's best for us.

<u>Mothers and Daughters</u>

Jessie knew that she was always under her mum, Anna's control. From a young age, Anna would use every form of blackmail possible to manipulate her into doing what she wanted. Losing freedom, love and pocket money were all basic forms. It was the lies that Anna told Jessie growing up that were what really affected her as an adult.

Jessie gave up trying to disobey her mother early on in life, because when she did, Jessie would find just the right type of blackmail to pull her back into line.

She couldn't think of a large life decision that she had ever made without her mother's approval. So when Jessie took a small business loan from Anna, she should have known it would come with strings attached. Within six months she had gained full control of Jessie's personal bank accounts – to the point where Jessie was forced to check with Anna for even small purchases.

When Jessie met her husband, Anna immediately disapproved and did any and everything she could to break them up, including boycotting the wedding, refusing to contribute anything to it, and emptying Jessie's accounts to reclaim the loan without any notice.

It got so bad that they left the country, but both Jessie and her husband Harry still harbour great resentment towards Anna.

Control is care gone wrong. When parents think that they have free rein to manipulate their children into doing exactly as they say, they may justify it by thinking they know best, but they don't. Not in this case.

Protection, Discipline

Related Relationships: paternal, maternal.

> "Watching your daughter being collected by her date feels like handing over a million dollar Stradivarius to a gorilla." Jim Bishop

In many family units, discipline is a shared responsibility between both parents. Consistent and appropriate guidance, correction and punishment are important for children. I recently overheard a conversation in the playground between two kids comparing notes about their dads as to who would win if a fight took place: "My dad could beat yours in a fight", "No way. My dad is tougher and stronger". Children like to feel safe - that their parents can protect them, and often idolize them, even when the parent doesn't deserve it.

There is evidence that fathers' stress levels rise as younger children's behavior worsens, and a response to this in an increasingly authoritarian parenting style (including physical discipline).[39] The implication was that this type of discipline creates other negative issues that later need to be rectified. Perhaps your parents beat you, and took it further than they should have.

A big aspect of the relationship we have with our fathers is that of safety. We all have a basic need to feel safe, children especially. It is the father who commonly plays this role in a family. He is their protector, and this is no small thing. When they don't, we'll probably need to work through some issues to do with fear.

Threats to Protection

Perhaps your parents threatened your security in other ways. By making changes in a child's life, parents can shake a fragile sense of stability. You may have moved a lot, and had to adapt to a change in friends, schools, houses, or perhaps for your dad's work. Being forced to reconstruct your life over and over is not an easy task. Your parents may have intentionally threatened your sense of security. Perhaps they would bring multiple romantic partners into the house on a regular basis, or evict you at short notice during a heated argument.

It often falls to our male role models to lay down the law, to let us know the boundaries. When punishment is consistently too harsh, it can scar us and we may find it hard to relate to our fathers if they were too strict. Perhaps we are overly security- conscious – putting an insurance policy on everything, being afraid in fairly safe situations, or freezing in crisis situations. These are all just symptoms but we're seeking the underlying cause. Fear is one of the red flags we need to be looking for as we dig deeper.

Provision

Related Relationships: paternal, maternal, romantic partners.

Children cost money. Sometimes parents are forced to be tight with the money they spend on their kids. Perhaps your parents were a bit miserly when it came to spending money at Christmas and birthdays, or showed favouritism toward a certain sibling. It is easy to feel that the gift reflects the importance someone puts on a relationship. When a husband buys his wife a gift, he often frets over getting it just right, because the gift is a message, signifying how much she means to him. It may be that you harbour a grudge at your parents for withholding provision. Perhaps they didn't send you to the school you wanted, maybe was piano lessons you really wanted. It could be that this has made you bitter, as you believed that it would have led to a different set of opportunities in life.

The Gift Worth Giving

Kim didn't spend much money growing up. She never gave money away, never shared anything and never gave expensive presents (if any). She believed she needed to be tight with how she spent her money because money took precedent over the people she loved. This included the money she spent on herself – even when shopping for basic necessities, she was known to ponder small purchases for hours.

On reflection, Kim realized her parents never gave her a gift she actually wanted. Because of this, she had come to believe that she wasn't worthy of gifts, because she wasn't worthy of love. As a result she focused on becoming generous towards both others and herself.

Identity

Related Relationships: paternal, maternal.

Having a model to imitate and emulate is essential for children to grow – inventing games to mimic the things they see adults doing. Parents often treat certain children in different ways, depending on whether they are a boy or girl.[40] Good parents treat their children in a way that tells them they are special, and give them the support to find out who they are.

When we enter puberty, it is common for us to attempt to answer the question - "Who am I?" Delinquent teens join gangs, others will dress and define themselves by what music they like, their hobbies, what they're good at, or the sport they play. One study of children from divorced families found almost every girl in the study desired to reconnect with their fathers in the early stages of puberty, even when there had been no contact. Many had step dads, but almost all attempted to contact their genetic fathers, hoping to rekindle a relationship:

> "Like little detectives, the children of divorce know their fathers' real records, their good and bad sides. But they do not, as a rule, draw the conclusions an objective observer would make from those records. Instead, they have a powerful need to

create a protective, loving father, one who would never intentionally let them down... they express their undying love for the man who has let them down as provider, role model, and as a loving, interested parent."[41]

Why is it that children are able to imagine a "good" father in their heads, despite a horrific track record? Because they innately need their birth fathers to give them something others can't – a sense of who exactly they are, a sense of identity.

The Search for Affirmation

Jason is what you would call a "people pleaser". One compliment from someone who matters to him, can keep him going for months, but more often than not, he often gets depressed about the fact that he didn't live up to others' expectations.

His biggest fan was, and is, his mum. As a boy, she would frequently heap praise on him. Her praise was nice, but he really just saw her as doing her job as a mum. His dad, on the other hand, was a different story. He didn't say much, and when he did it was mostly critical and disapproving. But when Jason's dad gave him a compliment, he remembered it. In fact, he still remembers every single one. His dad's words had shaped him more than anyone else's.

As he looked back on his life, Jason realised that he lived his life in the light of one question: "What would my dad say?" He found that there was something missing - that he really just wanted his dad to affirm who he was. And that was what he was still seeking, but probably would never get. So he started looking in other places.

This desire to make our dads proud is a common one. A father's words can be hurtful when they are abusive or emotionally distant as we mature. The words of our fathers matter to us, because the role they play in our lives is to affirm and encourage us. When we don't have a good paternal role-model, there may be a "debt gap" - perhaps expressed in anger and directed at ourselves, our fathers, the world, authority, men etc.

Actions need to match complimentary, affirming words of a father. If you were consistently let down by your dad, his words will have meant a lot less. Repeatedly disappointing a child will negate the power of a father's words.

Another story from "Second Chances"[42] involves Rina, a girl whose genetic father was lacking in many regards. At her first interview, Rina is fifteen, she is dressed in leather, chain smoking, dating a boy in a gang, taking drugs, and hates the world. Her teachers and counsellors declared her "aggressive and unmanageable".

When we return for another interview five years later, Rina is completely transformed. Dressed in a smart business suit, Rina is wrapping up a computer course. What changed? "...After Mom married Jeff, he took me aside and talked to me like no-one has ever talked to me before. He said I was going nowhere with my friends. He talked to me many more times, asking me where I was going in my life and where I would be in a few years' time... 'he put his money where his mouth was.' She sighs. 'So I went to junior college and got good grades. He was so proud of me. My mom was so proud of me.'

Rina reaches across the table and touches my hand. 'I want you to know this. Before I turned eighteen, I went to Jeff and asked him to adopt me. I knew I was going to be an adult, but I wanted to have his name. I talked to Mom first and she said to go and ask him. He said he'd be honoured. So then I asked my real dad. He said he'd be hurt, but he'd do it if it was what I wanted. I knew it was just symbolic, but I wanted it.'"

Rina found a father figure in her step-dad, Jeff, who showed her who she was, saw something beautiful in her, and coaxed that out with his words and actions. Rina's response is as insightful as it is beautiful. She decides to allow her step-dad to adopt her. Why? It is symbolic of who she takes her identity from – the name is just the icing on the cake of the many other ways in which he helped her to discover who she was.

Companionship

Related Relationships: peers, romantic partners.

Companionship is a big factor in a healthy romantic relationship. It's easy to mistake the sizzle of physical attraction, for an emotional connection. Although without friendship, many romances don't stand the test of time.

> ### Losing Your Best Friend
> John struggles being a widower. He lost his wife and best friend to cancer 7 years ago. He even talks to the urn that her ashes are kept in frequently. John is excruciatingly lonely.
>
> John regularly pays for prostitutes to keep him company at night. For John, it's not about the sex - he doesn't have sex with them. Mostly he will have them read to him, and then hold him as he falls asleep.
>
> It's about the companionship. The thing he longs for, more than anything, is feeling someone's breath on his neck when he's waking from sleep. And having someone to talk with, and share with.

It's the little things that we miss about a companion. Dogs, commonly referred to as "man's best friend", are loyal, loving companions for people the world over. They don't say anything, but when they're gone, it's the little things we miss - the way they would nuzzle, or when we took them for a walk. A lot of the things that dogs do are qualities we value in our peers, but rarely find; not least among these is loyalty.

The same can be said of friends. Perhaps it's a friend who has left your life, due to distance, discord or death. Even if you hate them, you may still miss them. That's okay and completely natural, even though you wish you didn't. They can often add to our lives in intangible, unrecognizable ways. It may be that you're just really sentimental, and find it hard to let go of friendships for one reason or another.

Loyalty and Trustworthiness

Related Relationships: peers, romantic partners.

Trustworthiness is essential for relationships we can depend on. It may be that a close friend said or did something that breached our trust. In a marriage, the most obvious example is unfaithfulness. It may not even be an affair; it might be that a partner looks outside the marriage for their emotional and physical needs because they aren't receiving it in his marriage. When the betrayal is revealed, trust may never be fully restored. Yet with forgiveness and a proper reconciliation process, hopefully it can be a possibility if they're genuinely repentant.

When You Want To Forgive

Jessie and Harry were trying for their first child for many years unsuccessfully. When they finally fell pregnant, the sex was difficult both during and for a long time after the pregnancy. In between the broken sleep and the severe discomfort that Jessie was experiencing, intimacy was pretty much impossible.

Harry was working long hours and then coming home to a chaotic home life where he didn't feel loved anymore. Harry was angry that his physical needs weren't being met. So when the opportunity presented itself somewhere else, he caved in. An attractive co-worker made blatant advances, and they began a brief affair. Harry soon confessed to Jessie. They immediately separated.

Jessie just couldn't forgive him, however hard she tried. After a few tries at counselling they ended the marriage. Jessie wanted to forgive Harry – and still does. However much it made sense to forgive him (financially and relationally), she just couldn't. The feeling of betrayal was so great.

The last thing Harry wanted was for it to be over; neither did Jessie and nor did their new-born child. Nor did their bank balance. Although the barrier created was due to Harry, the barrier preventing the repair was

Jessie's inability to forgive Harry. Jessie didn't think she ever could, and didn't know how. Her head could probably see that it made sense, but her heart would never let her.

Forgiving Ourselves

One party we cannot forget is ourselves. The debts we owe ourselves fall into two categories:

Guilt: You did it and you were at fault. Your actions wounded one or more people (this may include you).

Regret: You let it happen, you had the power to stop it, but you didn't. You could have prevented one or more people from getting hurt, but you didn't (you may have been unaware of or have done it unintentionally).

Forgiving yourself can be the most difficult of all types of debts. It takes discipline and focus to account for the deficit, and forgive it. You can't be lazy, or allow yourself concessions, as your heart will still pursue the debt if you give yourself a "staff discount". If you have hurt others, or yourself, you may end up developing the same negative emotions, thoughts and behaviour of a victim. You can experience both guilt and shame at the same time.

If we are to successfully forgive ourselves, we need to start by finding reasons why we're worth loving. When you discover this, you'll soon work out why you are worth forgiving! If you don't believe the previous sentence about yourself, you've got work to do. Re-read the sections on finding value in others, and apply them to yourself.

Guilt: "I'm Sorry For What I Did"

Even if you are a mass murderer, you will have some kind of code or standard that guides the way you operate. In the Italian mafia, every gang operates according to a strict rule of "Omerta" - a code of silence ensuring loyalty to family. Even those with extremely flexible morals, have some kind of code they live by, however loose. When your actions violate your code, you may experience guilt. How aware of the guilt you are, and how you suppress it will differ depending on who you are.

Some people feel an intrusive sense of guilt. Perhaps it was a school or family member who used fear and guilt to scare you in order to make you conform to certain behaviours, even a religion. The word "morals", an old-fashioned word, but most people have things they will or won't do. The debt you create through the violation of your own code will be owed to yourself. It may be how you treat relationships, money, the environment, family, authority, and cultural taboos.

> ### Breaking Promises
> *Jason promised himself he'd never taste alcohol again. Jason was an alcoholic but he realized that his addiction was destroying his life. He promised himself he wouldn't touch a drop of liquor ever again, and made many promises and vows to ensure that he did so.*
> *Until he relapsed.*
> *Jason had one beer, which led to a three-day bender. When he woke up in hospital, he not only had to deal with the hangover, but the guilt of violating the promises he made to himself and others, and the significant damage he did to his body during this period. Until he relapsed, he could tell himself that he'd turned over a new leaf, and would never do it again.*
> *He figured it was a matter of time until the next relapse happened...*

Guilt can be a cycle: 1) make a mistake, 2) experience guilt and shame, 3) experience remorse and sorrow, 4) return to previous agreement, 5) repeat. It starts by doing something we said we wouldn't, then feeling ashamed because of this. We then make amends, vowing to never do it again and change our direction (repent), we "forgive and forget" the pain we felt when we were ashamed, and just as we start feeling good about ourselves, we do it again and start the cycle all over again. Your guilt may originate from struggles that only you have - desires that you're ashamed of, or an addiction that others don't know about.

It might be the impact your actions had on others. It might be the way you handled your role as a father, mother, husband, or wife. It might have been an isolated, singular moment that altered the rest of your life, or a whole lot of little moments that led to an outcome, which you really regretted. We've all done things we feel guilty about - mistakes are part and parcel of life. The real question is how do we deal with them, and how do we keep "getting back on the horse"? It has to begin by being fully accountable to ourselves. Although our heads will automatically want to let ourselves off the hook, our hearts will not let this happen. For complete forgiveness of debts to happen, we must listen to our hearts, not our heads.

When You Screw Up

Jason was married to Jem, an amazing girl who was everything he wanted in a wife. She only wanted to love him, and did a pretty good job of it, but he kept hurting her. Jason had some serious anger issues at the time.

In the middle of one of their infamous arguments, Jason completely lost it in a fit of uncontrollable anger. He lashed out, and hit Jem so hard that she was hospitalized for a week.

Jem left him.

Jason is now a broken man - a shadow of his former self – unemployed, sick, lonely, depressed. He has no hard feelings towards his wife – it is towards himself that he is angry. He still can't believe he could do that to another person. He can't forgive himself for losing the best thing he ever had. All he had to do was not screw up.

Once Jason recognised that his only hope of getting free of the guilt was by forgiving himself for this, and many other debts, he started making progress.

We can't 'un-sleep' with someone, 'un-murder' someone, or 'un-slander' someone. What is done is done. We may find that we do something – either calculated or in the heat of the moment, which we later regret, but something we cannot now change. We shouldn't try to explain it away with excuses. Face the debt, fully account for it. Then forgive it.

Regret: "I'm Sorry For What I Didn't Do"

Regret is what we experience when something is not done, that should have been (and usually is) within our power to. It may often involve other people or circumstances where we could have stopped a negative outcome from occurring and because we didn't, people ended up getting hurt (including ourselves). We may have been fully aware of the results of our actions. Or we may have been completely unaware.

When we are not aware that our actions are going to end in disaster, it's common to say "if only I had done … We replay it over and over again. It's okay to think this. Whatever our heart feels owed; we should fully account for, and then cancel the debt.

There is usually no way of having a second bite of the cherry when it comes to regret. That doesn't mean we have to carry it around like a chip on our shoulder for the rest of our life. The reality is that every person makes mistakes. Those who succeed, learn from these mistakes constructively. Neither guilt nor regret are constructive ways of learning from a mistake if we let them fester and hang around like a bad smell.

When You Owe Yourself

John grew up frequently being forced to watch his dad beat his mum senseless. The last time it happened he almost killed her. His dad fractured her skull and back, leaving her with minor brain damage. John replays these scenes in his head frequently, imagining himself intervening and rescuing his mum. He often thinks to himself "If only I could have stopped him".

The reality is that John was 12 at the time, and had no chance of stopping his dad. The only possible outcome was that John would also have ended up in hospital, or worse.

It has affected John well into adulthood. He doesn't know how to stop the feelings of anger and regret. He discovers that it's not just his dad he needs to forgive, but himself. He blames himself for his failure to act because he was afraid - even though there was nothing he could do to change the outcome. It was in this failure to act that John owed himself a debt.

Forgiving Institutions

It's easy to be let down by institutions. An institution can owe each of the qualities we expect from a person. Perhaps it was 'care' that we weren't properly given by a hospital or the poor teaching we received at school. Perhaps it was a government or bank we believed was going to protect us, but failed to. Perhaps it was a religious organisation that failed or hurt us. Institutions are there to meet the collective needs of people within a society. When they fail to do this, they fall short of expectations. We have to go about forgiving an institution (or a person within an institution) in the same way we forgive people.

Forgiving God

What we believe about how and why we are here on earth makes a huge impact on how we live our daily lives. Or putting it another way: believing that a deity made us for a purpose will significantly affect our decisions.

Whenever a terrible thing happens in the world (especially related to natural disasters), the first thing people ask is "how could God let this happen?" The conclusion we come to depends on the type of god we believe in. Is our god an angry and vengeful God? Or is he a loving and caring God? It is possible to reconcile the fact that terrible things happen and still believe in a good God. Many people, when faced with this choice, opt out altogether and choose to stop believing in God entirely, saying they refuse to believe God would let bad things happen, which is understandable. We may not be able to believe in a god who lets us suffer when he has the power to stop it. It is almost as if the decision to stop believing in God is retaliation for the things we believe he has allowed to happen.

Chapter 6 Exercises

<u>Table 1: Guilt and Regret</u>
On the 'Forgiveness Worksheet', click on the 'Forgiving Yourself' Tab. Print it out and fill it in in the same way you did on the 'Forgiving Others' Tab..

This table is different to the others, but is closely related to the others, so should be fairly straightforward

Work through the first 4 columns; allow room for columns 5 and 6, which we will look at in the next chapter. Come back and fill them in when you have read Chapter 7.

How do you feel now that you have completed the worksheet? Better, worse? Why? Journal about this.

Is this how you usually feel when you think about these subjects?

Chapter 7: The Forgiveness Method

Sometimes, just knowing HOW to forgive is half the battle.

I overheard a conversation when I was at the mechanic's the other day:

The mechanic was removing the cylinder head from the motor of a car, when he spotted the owner. They started chatting, and it turned out he was a world-famous heart surgeon. The heart surgeon was standing off to the side, as he had come a little early. The mechanic straightened up, wiped his hands on a rag and asked
'So doctor, take a look at this engine here. I open hearts, take valves out, grind 'em, put in new parts just like you. When I finish this, it will work just like a new one.'
The doctor, wondering when he was going to make his point, stared intently into the engine. The mechanic went on 'so how come you get the really big money, when you and I are doing basically the same work?'
The doctor smiled, leaned over, and whispered to the mechanic,
'try doing it with the engine running!'

Be Specific

Forgiveness is surgery with the engine running. We too, endeavour to do surgery on our hearts while we are going through life. Just like surgery, we delve deep to rectify the underlying cause of the problem; we must be as specific and methodical as a surgeon.

Just saying, "I forgive everyone for being mean to me" doesn't work. It hasn't worked in the past, and it won't in the future - we need to go a little deeper, and be sincere with our intentions. Our heart needs a specific list if we are to finalise outstanding debts. Much of the time, this is the biggest challenge - once we get the specifics out, the rest follows.

If we are to get these outstanding debts out in the open, we first need to listen to our hearts. Working hard and playing hard doesn't leave much space for us to slow down to help the process. Usually when our heart is harassing us for an outstanding debt, our instinct is to speed up and ignore it and then numb the pain. To listen to it usually requires some slowing down and focus.

A Rolling Stone Gathers No Moss

"Courage is what it takes to stand up and speak; courage is also what it takes to sit down and listen" - Winston Churchill

We fill up our lives to stay occupied, often to the point when the only time we stop is to sleep. Being still isn't easy for everyone. We fill our lives with clutter to stay in constant movement, not stopping long enough to give a little time to listen to our minds and hearts. We may need to give something up for a time if it's getting in the way. We don't need to, but if we're not seeing much breakthrough, perhaps trying one of these might help? Some common ones are:

- Phone
- Caffeine,
- Alcohol
- Tobacco,
- Media: including TV, Facebook, YouTube, other sites, music, games

If we are surrounded by distractions wherever we go, then perhaps getting outside on a sunny day might be the tonic. Get out in the park on our own with a blanket, and lie there and listen.

When we do start to connect with our heart, we may discover that there are multiple debts arising from one action against us. For example, if someone maliciously gossips about us, we might find that they owe us loyalty, affirming words, love. we need to go through and cancel each one of these debts separately. This can happen on multiple occasions, each time digging deeper and slowly scraping out the wound. Forgiveness is a lifestyle. Each time we forgive, we're unlocking a deeper part of ourselves, and getting freer. We may feel like an idiot, but the results will speak for themselves.

Phone a Friend

You don't need to do this on your own. If you are like me and you're an external processor, you may find it easier for you to do this with someone else. Forgiveness often works best as a team effort, if others can be trusted. You might get them to lead you through the process or get them to ask the questions. You could possibly then swap. Perhaps you would prefer to find a friend who has read the book to follow the steps outlined below - read this book with them, or even start a group or book club, and take it in turns working through the issues that your heart reveals.

This is actually one of the concepts that caused me to write this book. I figured there had to be a better way for people to work through their issues than paying people thousands of dollars to maybe "fix" them. If two willing people with normal social skills "co-counsel" each other by taking it in turns, I don't see why they might not also have a chance of sorting out their emotional baggage. If you want to try this with a friend, or find tips on to how to "co-counsel", look at the resources page of my website.

I know the first time I really, completely exposed my heart to someone, it was one of the hardest things I ever did. Being really vulnerable is risky, and it might be a bridge too far for you. The technique works just as well on your own.

Remember, there is no pressure to "get it right". If nothing comes, you shouldn't just give up or beat yourself up about it. Allow your heart to be silent if that's what it wants to do. You may have spent a lot of time ignoring your heart. You need to allow yourself some time to tune in to your heart before you start to see results. This is a process that takes time and should not be entirely forced. Relax, learn to let yourself go, get into the passenger seat and let your heart drive. If you don't have an expectation of getting results, you're more likely to see something amazing happen.

A number of research studies [43] observed that even people who were really good at forgiving, and had done it many times before took a number of months to overcome a serious wound. Don't be disappointed if you don't build Rome in a day. Healing is an ongoing process – it takes time to unlearn habits developed over a lifetime. Once the hurt underneath is removed however, a lot of the anger will be next in line to leave.

No Preconceived Ideas, No Expectations.

It's so easy to think we know where we need to start. We have a pressing thing we just have to sort out ASAP. We might sit down with an agenda, as in a business meeting: "I need to do this, fix this, this and this before I pick the kids up at 4…" If we come without a preconceived plan of where we want things to go, we'll be pleasantly surprised as to where we end up.

Not everyone perceives what needs to be forgiven in the same way. We might hear it, feel it, or see it. We might get a combination of the above. When I ask my heart "who/what do I need to forgive?" it is usually a memory I get. I then proceed through the rest of the steps.

Always ask what's behind a feeling. If you get a general sense that you need to cancel a debt, but it's not specific, you may need to dig deeper. Ask your heart for specifics. When you've been doing this a while, you may find it's more natural to do them out of order.

The Process of Forgiveness

The following process is one I commonly use when counselling people through the forgiveness process. I've seen it work in many different situations with people from all walks of life. The process is merged from Cognitive Behavioural Therapy (CBT) as well as others. The idea is to help individuals challenge their patterns and beliefs and replace them with ones that are productive.
The actual process of forgiveness is simple and easy to remember, and usually done in the following order;

> **A) Measure the Debt**
> **B) Cancel the Debt**
> **C) Dig Deeper: Look for Truth and Lies**

A) Measure the Debt

1: Ask Your Heart Who & What You Need to Forgive

Question to ask: "Who do I need to forgive?"

If it helps, feel free to address your heart directly, as if it's a person. When you're first starting out, it's best to ask either who or what you need to forgive – something like "who do I need to forgive?" Feel free to try new things and find a way that works for you.

A person may have done more than one thing to hurt you, so you may need to go through this process many times. Make sure you use their name at every possible opportunity, use their second - even middle names, if you find this helpful. Remember, be as specific as possible, but if you can't remember their names don't let that stop you.

What if you hear nothing and you're just drawing a blank the harder you try? Relax, perhaps try swapping step 1 and 2 around.

2: What Did They Do To You

Question to ask: "What did .... do to me?"

You might know what was done to you, but you might not have a clear sense of who was responsible. You might have multiple people who are responsible for a single event, but aren't too sure exactly what it was. Once you know what was done to you, go about surgically removing them one by one. Break it down into who did what things to you, and work through the seven step process person by person, specifically dealing with each thing your heart shows you.

3: What Should They Have Done Instead?

Question to ask: "What should .... have done instead", (or "What did .... owe me?")

We are focusing on the debts we are owed. These debts are the ones your heart is owed, so it doesn't matter about anyone else here. It is also important not to make excuses or justifications for the person who owes us. A debt is a debt, however large or small it is, it's important to be accurate and honest. We can't fool our own heart.

B) Cancel the Debt

4: Forgive The Person/Debt. Let them off

Say out loud: " I forgive .... for ...., when they should have given me .... instead. I forgive .... , I release them , and let them off from any debt my heart feels owed.

Saying things out loud can be powerful. Spoken words have significance. There is power in the spoken word – it releases something when we speak things out. Often we think our words will have the same effect whether we speak them out, or think them silently in our heads in the same way we will read a book. Many self-help experts will say that you can change your life simply by saying out loud what you desire to achieve. In the same way that saying something each day sets you on a course towards your goal, speaking forgiveness out over and over again establishes a habit of forgiveness, which over time will be assimilated into your life and modus operandi. 'Speaking out' forgiveness increases the effectiveness of this process in your heart. It can't hurt, can it? Nowadays, when people anger me, I forgive them out loud as I walk away.

This step involves you making a statement out loud. You have all the information you need from steps 1-3 to complete step 4. Remember to speak it out aloud, with authority if possible.

5: Allow Your Heart to Heal

I give full permission for my heart to heal any wound I have received from this.

Emotional wounds fester and get infected when left untreated, it is common for an emotional wound to go unnoticed. A little anecdote: One of my friends has four toes on her right foot. Riding her bike barefoot as a child, her mum noticed there was blood on her foot. She hadn't realised, but she'd been riding around without noticing that the bike chain had torn off her little toe. As soon as she realised, she went into shock, and fainted.

When you recognise your body has been hurt, you're naturally going to treat it – stop the bleeding, disinfect, close and bandage the wound. When you are hurt emotionally, there is nothing on display to draw your attention to it like blood. There isn't always immediate, specific pain either, so it's hard to know what to fix. Emotional wounds can regularly go unchecked and therefore they can also often fester. Negative emotions are red flags you use to draw attention to what you focus on. If you feel angry, sad, fearful, focus on them, as each are the red flags we use to know what we need to work on. When you no longer feel upset about it, you know you've worked through most of it.

Some types of festering wounds are:

- Bitterness
- Resentment
- Hostility
- Uncontrollable Anger
- Gossip
- Theft
- Revenge
- Sabotage
- Fear
- Sadness

This is far from an exhaustive list. These are all symptoms, but not necessarily the root of its cause. As we're forgiving, we are removing the underlying causes that lead us to being unable to control our anger, our tongue, our actions, our feelings, our thoughts.

C) Dig Deeper – Look for Truth and Lies

I came up with a list of the top three most commonly told lies in the world today, see if you can add any others to it:

1: I'm fine
2: I don't have any coins

3: I've read and agreed to the terms and conditions

6: Look for the Lie

"The most common lie is that which one lies to himself; lying to others is relatively an exception" - Friedrich Nietzsche

"Did I believe a lie about something?" (About me, relationships, the world, God)

The next two steps focus on changing dysfunctional thinking and modifying beliefs and assumptions to change behaviour. Once we've done steps 1 to 5, and identified and forgiven debts - there is a deeper layer to dig into. Decisions we make are based primarily on assumptions, information, and experience. These are foundations upon which we order and live our lives. When we are hurt, we make adjustments to these assumptions based on this experience, so we need to unmake them to return to living our lives as we did before, uninhibited by fear, but not forgetting the valuable lessons we learned during the process.

Foundations are critical when constructing a building. If it is not founded on a base that is solid and immovable, it can crack, lean, or fall over. The most famous example of this is the Tower of Pisa. When the builders began building the second story, it began to lean because of the unstable foundations beneath. Work stopped for almost a century as the building looked certain to collapse. Eventually another phase was added to compensate for the angle, resulting in a final structure that curves. When the foundations upon which we live our lives aren't solid, anything we try to build may lean, or crack, or collapse entirely. Our only lasting solution is to address the issues with the foundation.

If we are to build things that last, we have to first ensure we are working with a firm foundation. Life is filled with the potential to experience hurt, offense, rejection, pain, and humiliation. We won't even notice the subtle shifts when it's happening. It often comes to our attention later on when we face a similar situation, such as trusting a person or doing something that we were previously burned by. When we react differently, sometimes illogically, we'll probably be left wondering why. Usually, it's an issue of trust – our assumptions have shifted without our noticing. This is the point when we come face to face with "the Lie".

Some people believe that lessons from the school of hard knocks are the most valuable. It's important to learn from our mistakes, but we also need to rid ourselves of the unproductive side effects – such as fear, anxiety, anger etc. It is through
knowledge of the past (mistakes and achievements) that one is able to become wise. There is an aspect that needs to heal through forgiveness, to let us make decisions with complete clarity of thought and without negative emotion.

How do we make repairs to our foundations? For us to really experience freedom in a new way, we need to swap the assumptions we recognise as untrue, for things we see as truth just as we would change a part in a car engine that needs replacing.

Types of Lies

We can often have a few unnoticed misconceptions about life. To adequately address each of these is a book in itself. Below, are a few common lies we may encounter. It will be up to us to discover what truth works for us.

The Rebound

Kim's new boyfriend is great. She thinks he might be the one. It's only the second week in, and they're already talking about marriage. Her friends keep telling her it's a rebound as she only just broke up with her fiancé. But how can a rebound feel so right? She knows there's things she needs to work through before getting into another relationship, but this is an offer too good to pass up.

Until six weeks in, when things get REALLY serious, and she completely freaks out. She tells him that she can't do it and it's all over. It ends messily.

She has had a boyfriend since she was 11, hopping from one to another until her early thirties. The benefit of being pretty was that there was always an interested boy somewhere. Somewhere along the line, there were a whole lot of lies she'd believed about herself. She realizes that there's things she needs to work through. That she is looking for her identity in the love she gets from her boyfriends. Without a man, she feels like a nobody. The only way she can work through this is on her own. She needs work out who she is.

i)   Lies About Ourselves

There are many lies that we assimilate into our foundations because of past hurts. They will be different for everybody and have a slightly different feel for each of us.

The English language is lacking when we want to be accurate in describing how we feel towards others, especially when using the word "love". When I refer to love below, I am using the term very loosely. It can be the bond two friends feel towards each other, people we "like", or a colleague who we are friends with. But it may be a lover, or parent, or sibling, who we would say that we love in a deeper way.

I Am Not Loved

If I roughly took the people I interviewed and divided them into people who really have a sense of worthiness ...(they have a strong sense of love and belonging), and folks who struggle for it – folks who are always wondering if they're good enough. There was only one variable that really separated ... and that was the people who have a strong sense of love and belonging believe they're worthy of love and belonging, that's it, they believe they're worthy... our fear that we're not worthy of connection was something that both personally and professionally I needed to understand better.
– Brene Brown[44]

The belief that we are not worthy of receiving love will be the underlying cause of most of the issues we have.

When we believe we are unable to be loved by others, of having others give us their love, we will feel that we are dysfunctional in some (barely noticeable) way. We are afraid to expose ourselves when someone does want to love us, in case they throw it back in our face. Fear of rejection is being afraid that other people will start believing the lie that we already have – that we're unlovable. Think of this in terms of a transaction – our ability to give and receive love. Our belief that the love we offer will be discarded or rejected is linked inextricably to believing that we are emotionally incapable of receiving love, or embracing the love of others toward us.

Most other lies are a version of this one. When we embrace the truth that we are wired and capable of giving and receiving love, our hearts will unlock in new ways.

One of my favourite theories on romantic love comes from a 1986 analytical factor study, the "Triangular Theory of Love"[45] which theorises that all relationships that involve romantic love can be broken down into three factors. It proposes that all romantic relationships can be analysed by looking at three elements: passion, intimacy, and commitment. It defined them as:

- Intimacy: closeness, care, support.
- Passion: emotional connection, physical arousal (sexual arousal and physical attraction).
- Commitment: requires a decision to love and maintain love over time.

Relationships between lovers can be high and low on different factors. Some of those that he highlights are "Empty love", where only the commitment factor exists. "Romantic love" is high on intimacy and passion whereas "Companion love" has both intimacy and commitment. "Consummate love" sees all three working together.

We have the capability to receive and give love in all three ways, whether we recognise it, or not. As our heart accepts this fact, we will start to be more sensitive to people giving us their love.

I Must Be Perfect To Be Accepted.

The perfectionist believes that they must be perfect to be loved. Anything less, and they have failed to be "worthy" of love, resulting in feelings of inferiority and rejection. They will ask such questions as, "What is wrong with me?" When they are rejected in some way, they then blame themselves. This seems to be a no-win scenario. They can only ever live up to expectations (perfection) but never exceed them, so often they're living in a perpetual state of disappointment at their failings. When someone rejects them, they believe it was them that didn't do enough to earn the person's love..

The Mark = Perfection

I Must Have Everyone's Love and Approval

By not caring too much about what people think, I'm able to think for myself and propagate ideas which are very often unpopular. And I succeed.

- Albert Ellis

The people-pleaser constantly compromises, hoping to please everyone, avoid offending anyone and be loved by everyone. They believe that to feel loveable, everyone must love them. When someone doesn't, it then confirms to them that they are not loveable. They'll go to great lengths to attempt to be popular and well liked, often unsuccessfully; instead they can end up being mildly liked by a majority. Achieving a goal is secondary to making sure no-one is offended. When a goal is in direct conflict with what someone else wants, they will usually sacrifice it in order to please the person. In its most extreme form, people may appear "desperate", and will often be taken for granted.

The Mark = Universal Popularity

It's Easier to Flee Problems Than Face Them

> "I am going to stop putting things off starting tomorrow."
>
> - Sam Levenson

When faced with a "fight or flight" situation, this person will run from a crisis. An "avoider" will procrastinate or flee an issue by ignoring or avoiding it. They may have been hurt by conflict in the past, so they find it stressful and will run from it at any cost. It is hard to have deep relationships without working through conflict and difficult issues, so they have few, if any. These people believe that conflict leads to rejection, so they avoid it because they are afraid of the outcome.

The Mark = Not Deciding Is Always The Least Painful Option

ii) Lies We Believe About the World

My Worth is Determined by My Performance.

From our first day of school, we are taught that WHAT we do determines WHO we are. Rewarding good performance has taught us that it is our success that affects the love we receive. The sporty, attractive kids are popular; the smart kids get the accolades. We also learn this from our parents. They may threaten their children to encourage them to conform – saying or acting as if they don't love them, perhaps threatening other penalties, or comparing them to a more "successful" sibling.

Learned Behaviour

Joe worked out pretty early on that the affection his father, Frank showed him was entirely conditional on performance. If Joe got good marks at school, did his chores and behaved, his father would tolerate him.

But if Joe got less than spectacular grades, failed to do be fastidious around the house or did something to upset his father, Frank would reject him, and say things that really hurt him. The thing that really stood out most in his memory from childhood was that every time he broke a drinking glass, he would burst into tears. Even as an adult every time he did this he would get upset at himself. In counselling, he remembered that when he cried, his dad would often be more lenient with punishment.

Joe couldn't remember a time when Frank had said, "I love you" to him or his three siblings. Most of the time his dad was a very hard taskmaster, and he suspected that was why he was so career driven as an adult – he needed it to feel valued as a person and subconsciously wanted to please him.

The reality is that humans have innate value apart from what they do, as discussed in Chapter 3.

It is the fact that we are human that determines that we have great value, not what we do.

The Mark = What I Do Is What I'm Worth

The World is a Dangerous Place

When we have been hurt by a random act, it follows that we will believe that the world is dangerous - that every time we leave the safety of our own home, the world is out to get us. Depending on where you live, this might be quite true, but we will still have to enter the world to work, shop, socialise, live. Experiencing overwhelming fear every time we do so is something we shouldn't have to live with.

iii)Lies we believe about people

Nobody loves me unconditionally
The love that we receive from someone often comes with conditions. Perhaps your partner married you for your looks, your money, or your status. Things are fine when you're holding up your side of the bargain – but the fear that it will all be taken from you leaves a nagging doubt in the back of your mind that your friends may disappear if other things do. Perhaps you suspect you may be hanging out with "fair weather" friends.

People only love me for what they can get out of it
According to transactional psychology, people love us up to the point where the benefits no longer outweigh the costs. If the relationship becomes too painful or costly for someone, they may end it. Knowing this, how do we trust someone in a relationship? Trust is the currency of every relationship. This is especially the case in marriage, we want to believe that both parties really meant the words "till death do us part". We may have a sneaking suspicion that they will discard us if a better offer comes along.

People don't value my love
When others don't value our love as much as us, it hurts. When it happens a lot, it's easy to believe that this is all you can expect in future. Perhaps they discard it, or are ungrateful for it. When we fall for this lie, we will take fewer risks, and expose our hearts less to the risk of hurt. We will also believe that the love we give is worthless, and hence, we ourselves have little value. Feeling unlovable relates to our ability to receive love. Believing the love we give is worthless is the other side of the same coin. Knowing the truth of both is key if we are to re-establish our foundations so that they can't be shaken.

iv) Lies we believe about God

If you don't believe in a God, you might want to skip this next section.

Closely related to what we believe about the world, is what we believe about the universe, and who/what made it (i.e. God). Addressing these may help us to increase the connection we have with God and result in a clearer motivation to cancel debts.

God's love must be earned
Many religions teach that we earn our way into God's good books through our actions; the flipside is that if we're not loved, we won't do the right thing.

God is angry with you
When we miss the mark, we may believe that God gets angry with us, and will punish us for it. We might feel led to do certain things to "pay" for it because we think that it's what he expects. The motivation is Fear - believing that because God is perfect, he expects us to be perfect too.

All my problems are caused by my mistakes
When things go wrong in life, some people will connect these events to seemingly unrelated ones. There are certainly consequences for our actions – we murder someone, we go to prison – but thinking that someone died because we stole a loaf of bread fifteen years ago is just silly.

7: Find the Truth

The word "truth" refers to the set of assumptions we live our lives by, and as such are mostly relative to us. There is a difference between "personal" truth and "absolute" truth.

Personal truth is just that – personal. It will differ drastically for each person and it will ultimately be our heart that tells us what to embrace, and what to let go of. Not every truth will be easy to accept or to take on board. We live our lives according to a set of truths, whether we are aware of them or not, which change as we progress through our lives, as we learn and experience more. They are our foundational assumptions about the world, ourselves, relationships and where we came from and determine the course of our lives far more than we may think.

Universal Truth

Universal truths are more like a series of laws[46]– gravity, physics, cause and effect, that day follows night, etc. The world is governed by certain laws that all inhabitants are subject to. In 2011, the Large Hadron Collider [47], which speeds up particles at speeds approaching the speed of light, thought it had recorded particles travelling at speeds greater than the speed of light. For a while, one of the foundational scientific principles - Einstein's theory of relativity - was called into question. This was later nullified, but the consequences would have been massive, as many scientific theories about the universe would have been disproven.

Finding Truth

"All truths are easy to understand once they are discovered; the point is to discover them." - Galileo Galilei

Everyone has different sets of values. Recognising that we have believed a lie is the easy part. Finding the truth is the more difficult task. It may be something that we haven't been listening to, which has just been swept under the carpet for many years. It is quite likely though, that we'll need to look at external sources for at least some of this. We might get a hint of what it is, but will need to do further digging to get the full picture. It rarely makes itself blatantly obvious, nor presents itself neatly packaged. Discovering truth will lead to us going on a quest, finding fresh sources and guides that we have never looked at before. We will need to open ourselves up to possibilities that we have never previously considered. If we are open minded, it will likely lead to us genuinely assessing a wide range of possibilities to substitute a previous "truth". It'll be easy to see why we think we are unloved, but harder to see that we're loved if we've never experienced it.

The Search for Truth

> God offers to every mind its choice between truth and repose. Take which you please; you can never have both. -Ralph Waldo Emerson

One thing we can't expect is to do nothing, and still find what we're looking for. If it isn't readily on hand when we ask our heart what the truth is, it means that we need to go out and get it. Remaining with the status quo, and not actively pursuing answers, won't see any results. To fix and stabilise our foundation, we need to make changes. Maintaining the status quo won't do that. You can't be told the truth, you need to find it and own it for yourself.

Truth Requires Honesty

> The search for truth implies a duty. One must not conceal any part of what one has recognized to be true. -Albert Einstein

Truth can come from a wide range of places. We can base our opinion on an expert's ideas, read a book or blog, or we can rely on our own experiences. It might come from a book like the Bible, or it might come from a science textbook. What you will probably need to do at some point is realize that the search will take you to new places.

8: Replace the lie with the truth

It might be useful to write down the lie and the relevant truth you want to replace it with. You might even want to write a list, and go through it line by line, saying it out loud on a regular basis. Last thing you want to do is forget it. In this manner, you will feel like you are accomplishing something. By crossing them out, you will feel a sense of relief and commitment to your cause. I suggest simply saying the following out loud, as you have done for the previous steps.

I exchange the lie that.........for the truth that........ I take this truth and base my life on it today.

9: Teaching others how to do the same.

Once you have this as a regular habit in your life, you may be in a place to help your friends. I often show people, in 15 minutes, how they can use these techniques to help themselves. I'll just write the above 8 steps down on a napkin, and get them to go home and try it. Once they learn the basics, you can sit down together and practice on each other. You'll have the tools then to show your friends and family how to begin getting free of their own baggage.

So just to reiterate, the steps are as follows:

1: Ask Your Heart Who & What You Need to Forgive
2: What Did They Do To You
3: What Should They Have Done Instead?
4: Forgive The Person/Debt. Let them off
5: Allow Your Heart to Heal
6: Look for the Lie
7: Find the Truth
8: Replace the lie with the truth
9: Teaching others how to do the same.

The statement in full is:

" I forgive ....[column 1]...... for ....[Column 3 - the wound]........, when they should have ....[column ...4 - the debt].... instead. I forgive ....[column 1]...... , I release them , and let them off from any debt my heart feels owed.   I give permission for my heart to heal from any wound that this has caused. I exchange the lie that.........for the truth that........ I take this truth and base my life on it today.

Follow these steps, and you're on your way.

Chapter 7 Exercises

Print another Forgiveness Worksheet (get it from Mykeyrobinson.com/downloads if you haven't already). Go back and complete both the 'Forgiving Others' and 'Forgiving Yourself' tab.

1. Are you good at being still? If not, what distracts you?

2. Find a quiet place where there are not distractions, switch everything you can off (phone, people, food/drink, noise, TV, computers etc.) You may feel some resistance from within. Remove all distractions including electronic devices (such as phones) and people.

3. Go back over your exercise sheet from Chapter 5. Fill in the last two columns and replace the lies with truth.

4. In this worksheet, look at the relationships you had with caregivers, mentors, friendships, peers and romantic partners (as discussed in Chapter 6). Work through columns 1 - 4 as you did in the previous chapter.

5. For each line of the this worksheet, read aloud the following statement, filling in the correct gaps: "I forgive ....[column 1]...... for ....[Column 3 - the wound]........, when they should have ....[column ...4 - the debt].... instead. I forgive .... [Column 1]......, I release them, and let them off from any debt my heart feels owed. I give permission for my heart to heal from any wound that this has caused."

In Column 5: write the lie (if any) that you believed. It might be about yourself, others, the world, god, and so on.

In Column 6: write the truth that you want to replace it with.

Say: I exchange the lie that...... [Column 6]...for the truth that....[Column 7].....

Think About It

Do you have someone you trust enough to help you work through this process? How would you approach them?

What do you expect to improve through this process? How do you think it will happen? Write these down.

Section 3:
How to Reconcile

Chapter 8: Hope, Fear & Clarity

It's not easy to recognise whether someone is really sorry.

A preacher's sermon one Sunday was titled "Forgive Your Enemies".
Toward the end of the service, he asked his congregation, "How many of you have forgiven your enemies?" All responded, except one small elderly lady.

"Mrs Jones?" inquired the preacher, "Are you not willing to forgive your enemies?"

"I don't have any," she replied, smiling sweetly.

"Mrs Jones, That is very unusual. How old are you?"

"Ninety-three," she replied.

Hoping to make a point, the preacher said to Mrs Jones "What a lesson to us all you are. Would you please come down in front of this congregation and tell us all how a person can live ninety-three years and not have an enemy in the world."

The little old lady tottered down the aisle, faced the congregation, and with a proud grin on her face, said, "I outlived 'em all"…

Forgiveness is a Lifestyle

"Forgive your enemies, but never forget their names."

- John F. Kennedy

Not too long ago, I played a prank on a friend. It was very funny, and we all had a laugh, mostly at her expense. The next day, we found ourselves in exactly the same situation. I offered her assistance the same way as the day before, but this time she responded "I am a good enough person to forgive you, but not a stupid enough person to trust you again." She probably had a point.

Forgiving someone doesn't mean that we have to trust them in that same way again. Forgiveness is free, but trust is earned. Trust can be lost in the same way it can be earned. If someone screws us over, wisdom says don't give them a chance to repeat the same mistake again. Trusting someone again starts with baby steps – it's wise to trust a person with small things before you give them big things again. They may let you down, and that way you'll have less at stake.

Mixing Business and Pleasure

Joe knew he should never have trusted Rich – 'never mix business and pleasure', he always said.

Joe did a deal with Rich after meeting him at church. Rich was well respected by the mutual friends Joe asked for character references. So he decided to bend his golden rule.

Rich however then turned around and ripped him off. After giving up seeking payment on the deal, and his friends from church siding with Rich, telling him to "turn the other cheek", Joe forgave him.

Joe always thought that forgiving him meant he should be able to trust someone in the same way again, so he did a similar deal with him a second time.

The whole situation repeated itself – Rich did it again, and in exactly the same way as last time.

Joe now experiences fear whenever he does a business deal. It often takes him overly long to make a decision. He has lost some of the best opportunities because of this. He also now has fits of rage at the first hint that someone might let down their end of a deal.

Forgiveness takes away the anger or bitterness we may feel towards people who have treated us unfairly, and allows us to eventually be able to interact with them and feel no ill will. We are also completely within our rights to NEVER interact with them again. The decision is entirely ours to make, but we won't be able to make it with clarity until we have forgiven the debt the person owes. They may claim that they are a new person and totally, permanently rehabilitated, but wisdom says that we shouldn't just take them at their word. There need to be certain signals there.

I can't stress enough how important it is to be wise here! Forgiving someone is not a licence to let them repeat what they did to us. It's no more fun the second time around. In chapter 3 we looked at the motivation to forgive based on a particular study of forgiveness factors. One of the key factors is age –older people find it easier to forgive, because they have less time left in life, and so we are highly motivated to reconcile. Young people, on the other hand, are less likely to forgive as time isn't short for them, and by not forgiving, it might protect them from further victimization down the track.

It's a familiar theme in Hollywood movies that two characters reconcile because one is dying. If there weren't a pressing reason to forgive, in reality it would probably be impossible to get them to forgive. For full reconciliation, both parties usually need to have a desire to change. If only one party has this, it can still happen, but having limited contact in controlled situations may be the wiser option.

The Spectrum

> If we open a quarrel between past and present, we shall find that we have lost the future.
>   - Winston Churchill

So what is the point of reconciling? Assuming that we have worked through the debts that the person owed us, why would we reconcile with someone, especially if they don't want to change their behaviour, or even apologise for what they did?

We may not necessarily choose to engage with someone in the same way that we did prior, but we may find it necessary to remain in contact with the person, as in the case of divorced parents. Our aim is to remove irrational fear or optimism so that we can make a decision on where to go with some semblance of clarity, allowing us to be able to function optimally in the present. Whether it is interactions in a relationship, a job, investments, with family or something else involving an unknown outcome we want to be unaffected by our baggage from the past so that we can decide what's best for us in future.

It may help to see this process on a spectrum. At one end is extreme pessimism, at the other, optimism. Somewhere in between these two extremes is a moderate and healthy place where we can hold the tension of the risk and reward of a decision without them growing too large that they obscure reality and biasing us toward one extreme or the other. Many schools of thought have similar theories around appetite for risk, including economics and psychology[48].

Pessimism: When we have been hurt in the past, it is logical that we harbour fear and anger towards the person who hurt us. Many people use this to protect from repeating the same mistake all over again. By removing fear, we may be lowering our defences.

Optimism: When our defences are down, we may swing past a point of optimum clarity towards being overly optimistic about how a person behaves, expecting them to treat us differently the second or third time around. If we are a particularly optimistic person, we may be taken advantage of repeatedly, as we too easily expect the best from people and result in our putting ourselves in a dangerous situation.

Clarity: Once we have come to terms with the potential negative and positive outcomes, we have a chance of finding a place in the middle where we can approach a situation without either of them biasing our decision making abilities. You may choose to re-engage with someone who hurt you in the past, but it will be from proof that the person has genuinely reformed, rather than stupidity or naivety. You may decide to shut down all communication with a person based on cold, hard facts rather than blind fear. By getting rid of the excess noise that they create, we can make a decision based purely on the signal, the evidence in front of us.

Glass Half Full Or Half Empty?

"A pessimist sees the difficulty in every opportunity; an optimist sees the opportunity in every difficulty." - Winston Churchill

What is your natural tendency – glass half full, or glass half empty? Are you naturally an optimist or a pessimist when it comes to trusting people? In one of my first jobs, I worked as a door-to-door salesman selling long distance phone deals. Paid only on commission, I could go 7 hours in the blazing heat without a sale, so I'd make no money some days. There were a few times where I worked all day without a single sale. Sometimes in the last hour, I would make a string of sales in a row after seeing nothing the entire day. It happened a few times this way, and I didn't understand why. I knew I was on a hot streak - I felt different, but I didn't know why.

Many years later, I realised the only thing that changed had been me. When I saw no results, I was approaching each door expecting rejection, becoming more discouraged as the day wore on. It got to a point where I dreaded every door, but when I made my first sale for the day, I began to look at it each door as an opportunity. This subtle change in my attitude regularly led to a string of sales close together.

Economic commentators often talk about the "bulls and bears". A bull is simply someone who is optimistic about tomorrow, a bear pessimistic. The best investors make investment decisions based on facts, not feelings; they make decisions based on the signals in front of them, not biased by fear or optimism. When it comes to deciding the best course of action in a relationship, we should aim to get to a point where we look only at the signals.

Signals

Poker players "read" each other to find other players' "tell" so as to know if and when a player is bluffing. The most common version, Texas Holdem, has limited available information – the cards, and the behaviour of other players. Players can bluff – pretending they have good cards when in fact they don't - or they can act hesitantly to disguise a good hand.

Good players use past actions to determine the style of other players around the table, but ultimately, it is the cards in their hand and the percentage chance of winning in comparison to other players, that gives them the best information. For the purpose of the analogy we will call it "the signal".

A signal allows us to interpret a set of facts in a particular way to draw a conclusion, and then act upon that conclusion. Poker players make a decision based on signals, not always successfully, as fear and greed can get in the way. Fear comes from past negative experiences, greed from overly positive ones.

In poker, and other areas where the stakes are high, there can be a huge amount of pressure to get it right. Pressure brings out underlying issues, which under normal, circumstances would not show themselves.

Unforgiveness: a structural issue

The Tacoma Narrows Bridge opened with much fanfare on July 1, 1940. It got its nickname "Galloping Gertie" from the way the deck moved wildly during windy conditions. This should have been a warning sign to engineers, because four months later it collapsed into Puget Sound under high wind conditions.

The structural faults in the Tacoma Narrows Bridge was discovered when stress was applied. In the same way, unforgiveness or the act of 'not forgiving' is also a structural issue that will be most evident when stress is applied. Painful experiences will influence our decision making process unless you have forgiven and rooted out the lies beneath. If we haven't done this, we may discover that we make bad decisions in high-pressure situations.

Dating and Relationships

"I'm not upset that you lied to me, I'm upset that from now on I can't believe you." - Friedrich Nietzsche

Dating is a good example of the fear and optimism spectrum in play. Those of us who have been in serious relationships will carry baggage from past relationships. Irrational fear may look like fear of rejection or relationship failure, an inability to commit or to form a lasting connection with another person. Irrational optimism might look like an inability to see a person's shortcomings in a relationship where one may get an unrealistic expectation of future possibilities (i.e. marriage), or taking things too fast, scaring the other person off.

When we fear loss or rejection, we will find it difficult to trust. Trusting another person with our heart, intimate thoughts, and desires, is hard when we've been hurt repeatedly. It may not even be past exes that are really the cause. Opening our heart again can be dangerous as it once again, becomes exposed. Implementing forgiveness as a habit can counter this, but the world doesn't stop being a place where people (like us) get hurt. We are going to need to use this skill again in future. In a relationship, if we can't open our heart to someone and trust him or her with whom we really are, the relationship will eventually fail.

Cold Feet

Joe and Rachel have been dating for 8 months and it's starting to get serious. Joe thinks she is everything he's ever wanted. He just can't yet convince his heart to agree. It has been the same story with every girlfriend he's ever had – eventually they all end because he can't put his heart into it.

He doesn't even know if he's ever been in love.

Joe is 38 and has never been sure in any of the relationships he's been in before. He knows it's him. He suspects it has something to do with his parent's divorce, and the many location moves he experienced while living with his mum growing up. Rachel is a catch. Joe knows he won't do better. If he doesn't get his life sorted out soon, he'll lose her like all the others.

Bringing People To Justice

Sometimes we should never trust the person who hurt us again. In some circumstances we may also need to consider whether we will need to bring a person to justice for the safety of others. It might require us to inform law enforcement, or other parties in a position to administer justice, to prevent it from happening again. Once we have begun the journey of forgiveness, we'll be on the way to an unbiased decision on whether further action should be taken. If we are still feeling a desire to see the person punished, we may not be in a place where we can make a decision based purely on the facts.

If the person who has hurt us, committed a criminal act, the main question you want to ask is "will they do it again?" In bringing someone to justice, we are seeking to alter their behaviour so that they do not repeat the thing they did to us again. We have forgiven them, and therefore the pain will hopefully have subsided, and the anger attached to a desire to punish will not be there. Sometimes though, the pain and shame that they feel, prevent them from going through the long and difficult justice process.

The decision will differ from person to person, but forgiving before we make it (if we have the luxury) will allow us to face the skeletons in our closet with minimum pain, anger, and fear that would usually come with it. It won't be a simple or fun process, but it will make the impossible possible and the world a better place as a result.

Dealing With Abuse

Abuse is one of the most serious types of offense committed. It can take many forms, and be so insidious that people may not even know that it is happening to them. There are many books that have been written on abusive relationships that deal with the issue much more thoroughly than we have time to here. Abuse creates a wound that may fester into anxiety, posttraumatic stress, low self-esteem, helplessness, and/or an ongoing hatred and resentment of our abuser lasting a long time beyond the end of the relationship.[49] It can be entirely unprovoked, and doesn't need to be physical at all. Most abusers tend to operate in more than one of the categories below:

Emotional Abuse

Emotional abuse is generally the most common type of abuse. It might include harsh criticism, blackmail, yelling, ridicule, swearing, public humiliation, verbal attacks. The abuser may treat another like they own them, or like an object. The abuser may blackmail them into accepting the way they are being treated, threatening worse treatment if they resist or bring in a third party. The abuser may use silence or enforce excessive demands to get them to comply with what they want. They may coerce or threaten something the person loves, such as pets, family, possessions. It may be that because of this, a person gives in and does something that they later experience guilt about.

Social Abuse

An abuser may restrict access to friends and family (most commonly this is a husband or boyfriend, or sometimes a religious cult). They may prevent them from going places on their own, or limit other freedoms, such as phone calls and social activities. The abuser may force them to move away from family and friends without consent.

Sexual Abuse

Rape is also a crime that can be committed within marriage. Some husbands believe it's their right to take what they perceive to be rightfully theirs if it is withheld, but in a good marriage, mutual giving needs to be reciprocated and implemented. Attempting to force a partner into sexual acts they don't want to do is considered sexual abuse. This includes when a partner is too afraid or unable to give consent.

Physical Abuse

This can involve shoving, hitting and violence, smashing or throwing things, choking, and murder. It can also be withholding access to treatment, or putting the person in a dangerous situation through sabotage or abandoning in vulnerable situations.

Seeking Justice

It may be that we have gone some way toward forgiving the actions of our abuser, but we are still unsure what course of action we should take. Should we prosecute? Should we ever re-engage with them or cut ties for good? Asking these questions may help to determine a course of action.

1: Does Your Abuser Have the Desire to Reoffend?

This is the litmus test to know whether the person is truly repentant for their actions carried out in the past. The question to ask is: If they were absolutely confident that they could get away with doing the same thing, would they do it again? Sadly, in the majority of cases, the answer is yes.

If a person makes some kind of meaningful reparations to rectify their actions, it may be a signal that they are genuinely repentant for their earlier actions. The word "re-pent" means to change perspective (or direction) in a meaningful way. Have they changed the way they see the situation (the people they hurt, the things they have done?) And, would they do it again?

Many criminal offenders are not "repentant", even after spending lengthy time in prison. Instead, they regret getting caught. It's easy to mistake truly repentant guilt for the remorse that comes with getting caught. This is an important distinction to make. How to determine this, can be difficult, as we may have little, if any, contact with the person. Seeking out the truth means finding the middle of the spectrum where it is only necessary to pay attention to the signals. Being too hopeful could well result in people getting hurt. Remaining overly pessimistic could lead to someone who is genuinely deserving of a second chance being raked through the coals again, and possibly the loss of other things such as a salvageable relationship.

It has been suggested that the way our abuser acts towards us can be a "signal" as to whether we will be safe and valued in a continued relationship with them[50]. Acting repentantly and attempting to make amends for their previous offenses are both valid pointers to someone who is less likely to repeat behavior. Depending on what they did, they should offer to make amends for their actions in a way of our choosing. If it was a betrayal of trust, (say for example, if they cheated on us) they may offer to allow us to access their emails or phone. They will be willing to accept reasonable consequences for their actions such as getting counseling or making reparations. Essentially, it's only their behavior, not their words, which will provide us with useful signals. It is okay to take a period of time to decide on the genuineness of the repentance, perhaps increasing trust little by little, just don't take forever.

2: Will Your Abuser Reoffend?

The offender may not be in a position to reoffend any longer, perhaps because of age, injury or situation. This is quite rare, but if they have no ability to access vulnerable people, seeking justice may no longer be necessary. They may be elderly or incapacitated, or perhaps the abuse happened when they intoxicated and the person is a reformed addict. They may even be in prison for another crime. You may still decide to bring them to justice, but knowing it won't happen to anyone else may be enough to help you find peace.

3: Will There Be Fallout?

In many situations, people who hurt us come from within our own social circle. They may have been close friends, relatives, or key figures in a community we are involved with, and they may retain many common links, even if we have cut ties with them directly. In some situations, we may find the majority of people side with the other person, resulting in alienation, isolation and criticism.

All Alone

Rachel lived in a small, close-knit country community. Her husband, Bill was beloved by everyone in town - a local councillor, and charity fundraiser. He was a veritable cornerstone of the community. He also constantly abused her physically and sexually.

When Bill discovered that his wife was planning on leaving him he attacked her - severely injuring her and breaking a number of bones. He then went immediately to the police station and pressed charges - falsely claiming that Rachel had attacked him first so he was acting in self-defence.

As Rachel was in intensive care with life threatening injuries, police quickly dismissed Bill's claims and put him up for attempted murder. But the damage to Rachel's reputation was done. It was perception that mattered – and public opinion was that Bill was in the right.

When Rachel was finally released from hospital she realised that the entire town had turned against her. Rachel was forced to flee and was ex-communicated from social groups after getting regular verbal abuse in public. Not only did she lose her husband, but her friends and some family too.

Chapter 8 Exercises

1. Are you more an optimist or a pessimist? Do you like taking risks, or do you avoid them at all costs? Are you a mix of the two? Where did you learn this?

2. Have you ever been so paralyzed by a decision that you couldn't make a choice? Write about what happened.

3. Have you ever rushed into a decision before properly doing your research? Write about what happened. In hindsight, did you recall a "signal", or warning sign?

4. Have you had a romantic relationship where fear or optimism affected the relationship negatively? Write about what happened.

5. Have you ever been abused before? How did it feel? How did/will you resolve the situation?

Forgiveness Exercises Review

6. Review each row in the Forgiveness Exercise dealing with other people, consider what reparations the person would have to make for you to feel like they wanted to reconcile with you.

7. Have you recently noticed feeling better (less angry, bitter, frustrated, more warm, open, able to trust) towards any of the people in the table exercises since you started?

8. How would your life improve if both parties were to be able to reconcile fully. Detail what exactly it would look like in a perfect world where anything is possible. What (if possible) would need to change for this to happen?

9. Did any of these people abuse you in the course of your relationship? What type of abuse? What would you do differently?

10. How likely are they to do it again if you reconcile with them? What would you need to see before you decided they had permanently changed?

Chapter 9: The Step Beyond Forgiveness

Forgiving your enemy IS possible

"Always forgive your enemies – nothing annoys them so much." - Oscar Wilde

Up until now, forgiving has probably seemed at least a possibility. So far, the goal has been to get us to a place of neutrality, a place of moderation, where we are no longer hostile or desire revenge. If we don't have a pressing need to be involved with them, then we don't need to. There is no compulsion to reinitiate a relationship with them, and in fact, this is where the journey will stop for many of us.

There is, however, a step beyond passive forgiveness, beyond returning to this place of neutrality where we are emotionally unaffected by prior wounds. A place where we can again enter into a relationship of trust, albeit moderated and guided by our wisdom. When we have implemented the process of forgiveness, and would loosely describe it as a habit that we do regularly, we are ready for the next step in the process - that of loving our enemy.

It sounds a ridiculous and completely impossible goal, even if we were to want to. From here on in however, we will look at how to trust and love our enemy – the very people who hurt us the most, and then look at how to repair a relationship – out of either necessity or desire.

Stepping Out

The previous sections have been about bringing us from a point of open hostility to a place of neutrality. A place where we neither enter into further conflict and hostility, nor do we re-engage with another party. We've been able to remain neutral and distanced, and use this as protection.

But there is a place beyond neutrality, a place where we intentionally reconnect with our enemy and re-enter into a relationship with them, albeit of a very different and healthy nature.

If we have applied the principles in the previous chapters, we should have a framework that will allow us to forgive most things, given time and distance. Unfortunately, time and distance is a luxury that many relationships do not afford. Whether it is an ex with whom we have a child, a parent who lives under the same roof, or a colleague; we are often thrown into repetitive bouts of conflict with them. Which means even if we are working through the backlog of past hurts which they've inflicted on us, we are constantly playing catch-up with every new clash we become involved in.

Don't let them dictate terms

In some situations, an enemy may try to take the initiative and be hostile towards us. It is our choice as to whether we let this affect us and then respond in the same manner. It may not be an easy choice, but it is always ours – and that cannot be taken away unless we let them.

Recently, I was in South East Asia working with an organisation based there. There was a man there who took an immediate dislike to me for no obvious reason. In the beginning he was rude and blunt. Behind my back, I would regularly hear slanderous things he said about me. I knew that I would have to have contact with him as we were both working in the same place, but I chose not to allow him to set the tone of these interactions. I didn't let him dictate terms and if I had responded in anger, I'd have been letting him take control. I did not want that. So I chose to be friendly, sometimes overly so, which annoyed him all the more. I went out of my way to compliment him, and treat him as I would a valued friend at every opportunity. I could see he had anger issues, and I thought I might help him if he came around.

I did not think he was dangerous. I later discovered this was a major miscalculation. As I was leaving the organisation, I discovered he had been seeking to put me in serious danger. His plan had been to take me along with his accomplices to a pizza restaurant where he knew the owner. He would then steal my wallet, and drive off while I was away from the table, and leave me to pay the bill. As I had no way to pay the bill, the restaurant owner was to call a policeman friend he knew, who would then arrest me and hold me until I paid his bribe (a common practice of police in this country). My imprisonment may have lasted weeks, and could have resulted in a criminal conviction and major financial loss. The only thing that stopped him was a friend, loyal to me, refusing to comply despite his attempts to emotionally blackmail her.

Why are they your enemy?

Our "enemy" may not understand why they have such an extreme reaction to us. A lot of the time it stems from envy or jealousy of things including:

Personality: it's nothing that either party does intentionally. Things that we naturally do, grate on them, and they react badly to it, harbouring grudges. This can often be the case for dominant personalities as they can overpower weaker personalities.

Position: we may be more senior, wealthy, successful, or have something else the person covets or begrudges us for. They have regrets, and may blame us for their wrong decision-making.

People: perhaps someone in authority liked us more than a colleague - a boss, a parent, a teacher. It's not our fault that we're likeable, but they seem to think it is.

Performance: Perhaps we are physically attractive, or good at something they want to be good at.

Past: Previous actions and events are often the cause of rifts between people. You may wish things had happened differently, but it's too late.

The best way to minimise the attention of our enemies is to avoid flaunting things we have that they don't. You could try to reach out to them – perhaps offer to help them get better at the skill for which they envy you, or angle for favour with an employer or person in a position of power that you have a good relationship with. Sometimes a simple gesture like this can resolve the entire issue, but make sure you are making the decision from a place of clarity.

Why Forgive an Enemy?

"Bitterness only hurts oneself... If you hate, you will give them your heart and mind. Don't give those two things away." - Nelson Mandela

Going that step beyond forgiveness can be costly in terms of pride and immediate self-interest, as it requires that we replace negative emotions toward the person, such as bitterness and vengeful feelings, with positive ones such as goodwill and sometimes even love[51].

Some of the most pertinent modern-day illustrations on how to forgive can be observed in South Africa and the move away from the apartheid regime.

Nelson Mandela was imprisoned by the government of South Africa for many years. He was later released and elected as president of South Africa. Mandela chose to attempt to unify South Africans of all ethnic backgrounds by encouraging true forgiveness and reconciliation after years of oppression, fear and murder. One of his first efforts was to ask the seemingly impossible task of the South African rugby team, the Springboks, to win the 1995 Rugby World Cup. He felt that winning would encourage South Africans of all races to unite, and see people of other races as fellow countrymen, not foes. Many black South Africans loathed the Springboks at the time, as they were seen as a symbol of apartheid.

In the movie Invictus, one of the most memorable scenes shows Mandela urging the National Sports Federation, the majority of whose members were black, to unite in support of the Springboks. He says

"Our enemy is no longer the Afrikaner... We have to surprise them with compassion, with restraint, and generosity. I know, all of the things they denied us, but this is no time to celebrate petty revenge."

Another powerful scene portrays Francois Pienaar, the Springboks captain, reflecting on their trip to Robin Island, the prison where Mandela spent twenty-four years as a prisoner. Pienaar says to his wife,

"I was thinking how you spend thirty years in a tiny cell and come out ready to forgive the people who put you there."

This is the question we want to answer. The motivation starts from understanding that in refusing to forgive, we allow the wounds we nurse to fester and the debts we are owed to accrue interest.

Nelson Mandela knew the risk of hating – in doing so we give them our heart and our mind. If we are giving our heart and mind to our enemies, then what is left to give to the people that we love?.

When we compare South Africa with neighbouring Zimbabwe, the knock-on effects become even starker. Unlike Mandela, Robert Mugabe, president of Zimbabwe held onto power at any cost - using hate and fear against the former ruling classes instead of generosity, forgiveness and reconciliation. This led to Zimbabwe ending up being a shell of it's former self with a failing economy, horrendous human rights abuses and citizens afraid for their lives and livelihoods.

South Africa would have gone a similar way if Nelson Mandela and his countrymen chose the same path. Mandela had many reasons to hate, but instead chose the less travelled path of forgiving.

Mr Mandela was not alone. Many ordinary people joined him in gutsy acts of forgiveness and reconciliation through the Truth and Reconciliation Commission, such as a Mrs Savage who almost died in a hand-grenade attack. She almost died, and could do nothing on her own – needing constant care to be bathed, clothed, and fed as she had shrapnel in her body that could not be removed. She wanted to meet the person who did it to her, as she wanted to tell him he was forgiven and to seek his forgiveness, adding "And I hope he forgives me also". Although she had no previous relationship with him, she wanted to reach out to him, not only to forgive him to his face, but also to seek his forgiveness for all that was done to him. She hadn't personally hurt him, but she sought forgiveness on behalf of her people.

What Does Loving Your Enemies Look Like?

"Do good to your friends to keep them, to your enemies to win them."

- Benjamin Franklin

When we love our enemy, we reach a place where we would freely help the person. We may not ever be in a situation (or choose to be) where we are called to do good towards them, but we need to believe that we would do so if called upon. If we have forgiven a person, we no longer feel the need to chase payment from them. We are no longer affected by what they did to us and neither do we seek revenge. We have no desire to have them involved in our life again. But what if they came back into our life? What would we do? How would we react?

This happened to me a few years ago. A girl that I had almost married turned up in my life again unexpectedly. Near the end of our relationship, she hurt me deeply when she started dating another guy behind my back. We cut contact after that, so I hadn't seen her for a year and a half and didn't know how I would react to her, but having forgiven her, I thought I'd cope okay.

She made a brief appearance in my social circle a couple of years later. The first time I saw her, I didn't get angry, I just thought, "you're dead to me, stay away". The second time, I just wanted to get away from her and never see her again, even though she was trying to act friendly as if nothing had happened. Not because I was angry, but because I didn't want to have anything to do with her

The third time, I was at a barbecue one night, and she unexpectedly turned up. She cornered me and asked me to help her in a specific way that only I could. It involved me reaching out to her in a way that I hadn't expected to, nor wanted to. Everything in me just wanted to flee.

I had a choice to make. Do I hurt her by withholding my help? Or do I give her what she was asking for?

I avoided her all night until she again cornered me. In that moment I chose to help her, even though I was very reluctant. In doing so, both of us were healed. A piece of my heart that was still missing was returned to me, and she experienced something similar.

This also happened to Corrie Tenboom, a famous holocaust survivor and Christian leader[52].

"It was in a church in Munich that I saw him, a balding heavy-set man in a grey overcoat, a brown felt hat clutched between his hands. People were filing out of the basement room where I had just spoken. It was 1947 and I had come from Holland to defeated Germany with the message that God forgives.

And that's when I saw him, working his way forward against the others. One moment I saw the overcoat and the brown hat; the next, a blue uniform and a visored cap with its skull and crossbones. It came back with a rush: the huge room with its harsh overhead lights, the pathetic pile of dresses and shoes in the centre of the floor, the shame of walking naked past this man. I could see my sister's frail form ahead of me, ribs sharp beneath the parchment skin... Betsie, how thin you were!

Betsie and I had been arrested for concealing Jews in our home during the Nazi occupation of Holland; this man had been a guard at Ravensbruck concentration camp where we were sent. ...

"You mentioned Ravensbruck in your talk," he was saying. "I was a guard in there." No, he did not remember me. "But since that time," he went on, "I have become a Christian. I know that God has forgiven me for the cruel things I did there, but I would like to hear it from your lips as well. Fraulein, ..." his hand came out, ... "will you forgive me?"

I had to do it — I knew that. The message that God forgives has a prior condition: that we forgive those who have injured us. I stood there — I, whose sins had every day to be forgiven — and could not. Betsie had died in that place — could he erase her slow terrible death simply for the asking?

It could not have been many seconds that he stood there, hand held out, but to me it seemed hours as I wrestled with the most difficult thing I had ever had to do. I had to do it — I knew that. ...

And still I stood there with the coldness clutching my heart. Yet forgiveness is not an emotion — I knew that too. Forgiveness is an act of the will, and the will can function regardless of the temperature of the heart. "Jesus, help me!" I prayed silently. "I can lift my hand, I can do that much. You supply the feeling."

And so, mechanically, I thrust my hand into the one stretched out to me, and as I did, an incredible thing took place. The current started in my shoulder, raced down my arm, sprang into our joined hands. Next, this healing warmth seemed to flood my whole being, bringing tears to my eyes.

"I forgive you, brother!" I cried, "with all my heart!" For a long moment we grasped each other's hands, the former guard and the former prisoner. I had never known God's love so intensely as I did then."

Corrie Ten Boom experienced healing when she chose to forgive a person who inflicted more suffering on her than most of us will ever see. I can tell you from my own experience, that finding the capacity to love your enemy is never easy nor is it always necessary. When faced with the important choice between loving them or hating them, I choose love.

Chapter 9 Exercises

1. Do you have any "enemies" at the moment? Why do you believe this? Have you let their behavior towards you affect the way you are treated?

2. Return to the tables on forgiving other people. Choose one person you are not fully reconciled to.

3. Do you feel that you were clearly in the right? How do you behave towards them now? (e.g.: cold, sarcastic, angry, bitter, etc.)

4. Assuming you had to reconcile, what reparations would the person have to make for you to believe they wanted to reconcile with you.

5. Using the following four headings, address how you would reconcile to this person:

A. How Close Am I To Forgiving?
Hopefully, you have already addressed this a lot so it will be quite brief.

B. How likely are they to repeat offend?
What would need to change to avoid this?

C. Have I Got Any Pride in this Situation?
Why do I feel this way? How can I overcome this to move on? Do I demonstrate any narcissistic tendencies?

D. Can I Make An Unqualified Apology?
Even if you feel you are in the right, and don't need to?

6. Looking at the worksheets you used to forgive, how did you fare? Do you feel released from the baggage you had before?

Chapter 10: Making The First Move

Practical Tips When Reconciling

Wade Frankum reached the rooftop car park of Sydney's Strathfield Plaza, blood spattered and breathless, he had already butchered his way to killing seven people, and injuring a further six with a variety of rifles and machetes. Looking for a quick getaway he scanned around, hoping to capture an unsuspecting driver to take him to nearby Enfield.

After concluding a brief trip to the shops to pick up a few items, Catherine Noyce was sitting in her car about to reverse out of her spot to exit the car park. She heard a number of loud noises that, to her ear was what she imagined might sound like gunfire. A figure covered in blood emerged from behind a van, brandishing a gleaming red machete in one hand, an automatic rifle in the other. It took her a second to react due to her shock. Her first reaction was to fumble for her half-open car window to close it before he got to her.

Eyes transfixed on the gun-wielding man, she felt for the button, and pressed it. To her horror, instead of going up, the window rolled the rest of the way down just as the man reached her car. She had accidentally pressed it the wrong way. Experts agree that this act saved her life.

Instead of blowing her away, Frankum asked Ms Noyce for a ride. He got into the passenger seat, and started confessing. Hearing the approaching car sirens Frankum apologized to her, got out of the car and fatally shot himself in the head.

Sometimes making the very move that the other person doesn't expect can completely disarm them. Oftentimes, the only way to rekindle a relationship is if we make the first move. As we forgive, we open up the possibility of trusting again in either the same or a similar type of relationship.

Hopefully, the outcome of this book doesn't stop at us feeling better about ourselves, and not sharing it with others. Ideally, this should be a process that starts with us, but spreads on to the family, friends and company around us. As we start to forgive, we will then be equipped to help others do the same. To do this we need to be the peacemaker - the person who swallows their pride and reaches out first.

Making the First Move

"Love is the only force capable of transforming an enemy into a friend." - Martin Luther King, Jr.

If we're expecting the other person(s) to make the first move, it's unlikely to happen. If we want to restore a friendship with someone, we'll have to be the one to move first – and be prepared for the pain if they reject us.

By going to someone and asking them to forgive us (even when we're completely in the right), we are beginning in them the process which we've already begun in ourselves – that of Forgiving. If you recall the "Franklin Effect", by asking for someone's forgiveness, we're asking them to do something positive towards us. By offering them the opportunity to forgive us, it forces them to ask the question "do I forgive them?" Keeping this in mind might make swallowing your pride a little easier (although it will never be easy).

The same motivations for wanting to pursue forgiveness are also true in the process of reconciliation. When a person has a desire to forgive, they are less likely to damage a relationship through anger, avoidance and bitterness. We may need to sharpen our motivation before we seek reconciliation.

If you are a bit hazy on finding motivation, or feel no desire for reconciliation, but know it will be necessary, you may want to re-read chapter 3. It may also be helpful, in some situations, to involve a third party respected by both people as neutral and fair.

Cancel Your Desire to Be Right

It may be that we felt we were clearly in the right? If we have a strong sense of inbuilt justice, we will need to forego our desire for an apology. It may come, but it may not; and seeking one will probably lessen the chance of reconciliation. If we go seeking peace but at the same time hope to re-engage over an old dispute, we will fail in our attempts at making peace. This includes "getting the facts straight" and other such misguided concepts.

There may have been no acknowledgement of wrongdoing, or even recognition of the realities of the situation. When we've forgiven fully, we will have let go of the need for other parties to know how things were.

Work On Your Manner

A lot of the time, we may be saying one thing with our words, but communicating another with our actions. Body language is vital. If we snarl "I am sorry", fists balled up in fury, we'll more often than not receive a similar response. If we're at the point where we have let go of the debts in our heart, we hopefully won't have much anger left.

There are, however certain behaviours we can employ to maximise the chance that a person will be receptive to our advances for peace. Here are a few ideas that might be worth looking into in greater depth. These skills will help you in any situation where conflict is involved, whether it's a street fight or an office meeting.

Ask Open Ended Questions

"Anybody can become angry - that is easy, but to be angry with the right person and to the right degree and at the right time and for the right purpose, and in the right way - that is not within everybody's power and is not easy."

- Aristotle

An open-ended question is where the answer can't be "yes" or "no". It compels the answerer to engage, to share their position, and their motivations and justifications behind these. Questions beginning with how and why are my personal favourites as they rarely end in a one word answer. You could try asking: "How does somebody feel or think about a situation?" to begin with.

Silence

Don't jump right in after they've finished speaking, and don't interrupt them, even if what they're saying is unfair. Let it sit for a while. Give them space to add to what they've just said. People process at different speeds - some will add thoughts after they've finished their initial response, and others will volunteer more with an uncomfortable silence. This is often the moment when people volunteer valuable nuggets of information; so don't hurry on too quickly.

Listen and Reflect

"Seek first to understand, then to be understood"

- Dr Stephen R Covey (7 Habits of Highly Effective People)

Listening before we speak is important because it will oblige them to eventually listen to our point of view (most of the time), and it will help us to couch our point of view in language which they will most likely understand and is least offensive to them. It will provide further valuable insight into their thought processes. Don't just wait for the other person to finish so you can speak.

After you think you've got a good grasp on where they're coming from, demonstrate what they have just said by repeating their answer in a different way. Attempt to summarize what they just said in a sentence or two. You may respond, "So you felt hurt because of the way I responded to." When they affirm this, you know you're on the right track.

Body Language/ Tone of Voice

Reaching out to the other person with a sympathetic tone of voice is important. The person may be suspicious already, or expecting us to attempt to start another argument. Our body language and tone of voice need to communicate that we are there to reach common ground and seek peace. In successfully communicating this, some of their barriers will hopefully come down.

Be careful that you do this in a very subtle manner, so they are not aware that you're doing it. Common body language techniques include:

- Open hands
- Uncrossed arms and legs

- Leaning towards them
- Reaching towards them, palms up

If the disagreement gets heated, don't mirror but sit or stand facing in the same direction while avoiding eye contact.

Eye Contact

In some cultures, regular eye contact communicates active listening, in others it can be perceived as a challenge and sign of disrespect. It is beneficial to know what meaning or message your eye contact is conveying to the other person. More so if there's a cultural divide.

Elements of a Peace Treaty

At the end of the Second World War, the victorious Allies forced the defeated Axis countries to negotiate a peace treaty. These included war reparations and new territorial borders. We too can learn valuable lessons from peace treaties, which usually include the following elements:

- Formal designation of boundaries.
- Processes for resolving future disputes
- Access to resources
- Status of refugees
- Settling of existing debts
- The re-application of prior treaties

Essentially, these elements set boundaries and guidelines for interaction between parties and account for changes to the previous relationship. Even the most bitter of enemies are forced to interact because they have a shared border. In the same way, many of us will need to continue to relate to our enemies because we share things like a surname, children, a fence, a house, a workplace.

You might want to discuss how you can negotiate use of shared property, rules of engagement for future conflicts, any outstanding debts (both literal and emotional), and other affected parties such as friends and family.

Going Beyond Switzerland

The Swiss are famous for their ability to remain neutral during regional conflicts. A peace treaty will only bring us to a place of neutrality. The process of forgiveness is part of this, but many studies[53] found that decreased negative emotion (such as retaliation and vengeance) isn't enough to repair a relationship. We will probably still remain cold towards the person, keeping them at arm's length to protect from more potential pain.

The forgiveness process (especially in close relationships) is complete when we return to a state of feeling some form of goodwill toward the people who hurt us. Nowhere is this more on display than in romantic relationships. In the context of unfaithfulness, partners who were able to forgive and experience feelings of goodwill toward the cheater had much higher levels of relationship satisfaction. Forgiveness sets the stage for reconciliation by short-circuiting the desire for revenge.

When You Have to Relate to Someone

There are times when we are forced to continue to relate to someone we'd prefer to never see again. Future interactions with this person can be at best awkward; at worst extremely painful. In this situation, forgiveness is a means to an end – that of reconciliation and re-establishing the relationship.

When someone is no longer in our life, our past stays in the past, allowing us to deal with it at our leisure - it may not be easy or quick, but it is stable. When we're forced out of necessity to continue contact with the person every day, they may add to the complications with each new interaction.

Being forced to face someone who is wounding us daily creates a number of other challenges. Every time they hurt us, it adds an extra layer on top of the original wound. Space and distance can give us some perspective to process and choose a clear course of action.

Forgiveness is a habit. If you can apply forgiveness here in the heat of the moment, you can do it anywhere. When you need reconciliation, perhaps doing the following as soon as you can might help. It is here you will become aware of how much has filtered through from your head to your heart.

1: Forgive

Hopefully you'll have a good idea of how to do this by now. If not, refer to Chapter 7: The Forgiveness Method. The goal is neutrality, while reducing and eliminating the feelings of anger towards the other person.

2: Assess the Situation

Do this prior to each re-engagement with your transgressor. As we forgive, we will have less anger and fear towards the other person; we will be able to get a clearer idea of the current status of things, and how to move forward. It may be that full reconciliation exposes us to further betrayals of trust. Perhaps there is a medium where we can have limited contact with them (given the right boundaries/penalties), with the aim of working towards a full reconciliation?

Forgiveness doesn't necessarily require us to trust in the same way as we did previously. Necessity may require us to forgive, but some tweaks may help to set boundaries on future interactions. When the anger subsides through forgiveness, we will be in a better headspace to decide what these are.

Beware Repeat Offenders

If it's not the first time, we will find it harder to forgive. We may feel frustrated or betrayed due to the repetitive nature of their actions, and the effect of forgiveness will be increasingly nullified with each offense. There may be a lack of accountability to motivate a permanent change of behaviour, and each time it happens, we will find it harder to trust and forgive.

Reflecting on the negative methods that are used to deal with conflict in the relationship will help us see possible changes that need to happen, and anticipate what the other person will say.

To determine the changes we want to take place in the relationship, we first need to identify the destructive communication methods being used.

If there is no agreement on your (reasonable) non-negotiables, it may be that you will want to remove yourself from the situation, as it's probably dangerous for you to be there. Remaining in the context of repetitive negative behaviour can often come at a significant cost and risk. Without repentance, a repeat offender will probably have little intention of reforming permanently. So if it's a serious issue, permanent conclusion of the relationship should be considered as it may be the most viable option.

3: Recognise Your Pride and Ask Forgiveness

Pride can often prevent us from taking the best course of action. Most people feel that being right is more important than being reconciled. It may feel better now, but perhaps not in the long term. Reconciling with a colleague or family member rather than having them gossip behind our back repeatedly will hopefully stop it spiralling out of control.

Pride is what gets between us and immediately seeking to be reconciled. Recognizing why we don't want to ask for a person's forgiveness will help us overcome our pride. It's rarely as simple as saying sorry when reconciling but it's usually where it begins.

Here are some common ways to recognise if we need to look at our pride:

- We are readily offended, eager to save face and will defend our rights vigorously.
- We unreasonably exaggerate the debts we are owed, especially when interacting with the other party.
- We are unwilling to cancel even small debts without full repayment (and in the manner we believe we are owed).
- We place an overly high value on self-assertion, and "face saving".
- We come out of an encounter thinking that we probably said too much and/or went too far.

If any of the above traits strike a chord, a truthful assessment of where we are currently is important.

KISS and Make Up

A stiff apology is a second insult   — G. K. Chesterton

By already having forgiven a person we will be able to approach that person without being hostile. Often it will be us making the first move - hopefully we'll be able to sincerely mean the words "Can you please forgive me?"

One study[54] looked at what the most successful method of apologising was. They found that a simple apology with very little explanation and detail worked the largest percentage of the time. This fits with the concept that an unconditional apology, with no caveats or justifications, is least likely to inflame a conflict further. The study also found that certain offenses required certain types of apology, and sometimes complications arise from a "mismatch" between misdemeanour and apology. In essence, we should keep the acronym "Keep It Simple Stupid" or KISS as we work up to an apology. Based on your assessment of the situation, we'll be able to custom tailor our apology. It's worth deciding what to say, and what not to say. Honesty is the best policy. But remember, words are like bullets – you can't take them back. So take some time to think about what, when and how you're going to approach the subject.

4: Wait Until They're Ready to Talk

It takes everyone time to cool down, but we often do it at different rates. If someone is able to move on quickly, they have to learn to work at the rate of others who aren't able to do so. It may be hard to wait, but it might be weeks before the other person is ready to communicate. Do this too soon, and we may find ourselves having a new altercation.

Keep in mind the way that some people deal with conflict can vary greatly. Whereas one person will confront every small issue directly and forcefully, another will refuse to address it until they explode (passive aggressive behaviour). These behaviours are often influenced by culture and background. Be aware of the person's way of dealing with conflict, as you will need to tailor your approach.

The End of the Rope

Kim's marriage was on the rocks. Her husband Dan was depressed, but refused to see a counsellor. They separated short term and it looked like he was getting progressively worse. Kim was quickly losing hope of any chance of reconciliation between them.

The last time they saw each other it ended with him claiming that he wanted a divorce (he had never said this before, so he may have meant it). He left the country to get some perspective, and she was left with their kids.

He was clearly the one most at fault but what she wanted more than anything else was to get him back. She knew that she'd have to make the first move and forgive him. When she felt she could mean it, she called him and asked his forgiveness. He wanted to try again, so she said it had to include counselling, both for the relationship and him on his own. All this was made possible after she had first made peace. They're now happily married

---

Forgiving in Broken Families

Divorce and separation is very common in today's modern world. If you have experienced it first hand in a broken family – either as a child or a spouse – you are in the majority. In every case, there will be an impact on the development of boys and girls, even if it's subtle.

Children are born with expectations of both parents. When these aren't met, there's a debt. If we can recognize the situation our parents faced as they tried to parent in difficult circumstances, we'll build empathy and be able to forgive them. Some people may not have any connection with their birth parents but it's important to recognize that birth parents owe us a debt, even though we may have little contact with them and as such they too, are an important party to consider in the forgiveness process.

Children of Parents of Broken Families

Studies[55] show that children have issues during and after a divorce because their needs are often put on hold by the parents as they struggle to rebuild their own lives. Loving fathers may abandon their children out of guilt or a desire to move on, and good mothers neglect children due to new financial and/or relational burdens. Children obsessively follow the lives of their parents motivated by a single gnawing question "Do you love me and even care about me?"

These studies observed children of divorce at various stages in life, and found that they typically experienced a number of side effects depending on the stages in life:

- They frequently harboured anger at the parent who initiated the divorce;
- They intensely longed for the absent/ infrequently visiting parent;
- They maintained a desire to reconstitute the pre-divorce family "if only my parents got back together";
- Over one in three had moderate to severe clinical depression;
- They often clung to fears of betrayal, abandonment, and rejection;
- They had earlier ages of initial sexual contact on average than kids from families that were intact;
- Delinquent behaviour was more common.

In their late teens and early twenties, these same children frequently experienced:

- Increased anxiety about their parent's divorce;
- An exceptional vulnerability to the experience of loss;
- On-going anger, resentment, and hostility;
- Depression;
- Low levels of life satisfaction;
- A reduced ability to maintain supportive platonic and romantic relationships;
- Had poor relationships with their fathers (65%);
- Poor relationships with their mothers (30%);
- Dropped out of high school (25%);
- Received psychological help (40%).

As fully-grown adults, these children experienced further side effects. When compared to adults who didn't experience divorce growing up, they demonstrated:
- An increased likelihood to divorce as adults
- A fear of repeating their parents' failure to maintain a loving relationship
- A fear of commitment and intimacy
- Less trust in their future spouse
- Reduced inhibitions toward considering divorce as a solution for marital issues
- Lower socioeconomic status
- Feeling less affection for parents
- Having less contact with parents and receiving less assistance than other adults
- Were twice as likely to exhibit these problems as youths from non-disrupted families.

Our parents have a lot to answer for. We may feel overwhelmed at times, but if we take it a step at a time, and do it in bite-sized chunks, we will make progress. Taking those first steps, in any walk of life, is the most important and difficult step. From then onwards, you will find that routine and consistency is the most important thing.

Children Towards Fathers

A child's relationship with the parent who doesn't get custody (usually the father) after a divorce is just as important as a continuing relationship with the parent who does. The relationship between children and their parents really impacts on them as they mature. Children of divorce don't discard their relationship with their father, even when a loving stepfather comes on the scene. There is a growing body of evidence highlighting the important influence of fathers on children throughout childhood and adolescence.[56] Many children experience a stage in their maturation where they desire to reconnect with their fathers, even after years of silence.

What fathers do and don't do impacts a child - whether or not they move away, start new families, or rarely visit. Fathers remain a key figure in a child's life, well after the divorce papers are signed.

Fathers remain a central presence psychologically in the lives of their children after a divorce - affecting their emotional life, self-esteem, self-image, and relationships. In one study[57], every child but one, attempted to get to know their real father during adolescence. Without regular access to their father, almost 75% of children felt   distanced and rejected by them, while the majority of the same fathers when surveyed, felt they had done sufficiently well. This disparity can be explained by the expectations of children when compared to the reality of the breakdown in a family unit. One result of the study found that it was not as much the frequency of visits, but the continuation of relationship where a child feels loved and valued.

A father will often need space in the aftermath of a divorce, when dealing with the overwhelming wall of emotions. If we had a father who found it difficult to communicate that he loved and valued us, we will probably be angry at him. Perhaps our father did attempt to communicate this, but his absences and inconsistent manner in the way he treated us resulted in resentment. Perhaps we blame our father for other factors that impacted on our development – poor marks, lack of direction, delinquency and poor life choices made motivated by a desire to gain attention, approval and love from him.

One subject not sufficiently covered in this book is sexual abuse in families, the majority of which happens at the hands of fathers or stepfathers. I hope this book may have helped you in some way; you may probably want to get further counselling about this issue if you haven't already.

Children Towards Mothers

Most children of divorce live with their mothers. This leads to a distinctly different set of challenges when compared with those living with their fathers. Children may be less aware of the suffering that fathers go through during the divorce, as they no longer live with them, but are usually aware of the issues their mothers face.

Where a mother isn't doing so well, a female child may make sacrifices to support their mother who isn't coping. They will take up slack in household chores, look after younger siblings and spend a lot less time with friends. They may develop extremely close friendships with their mothers and take on the role of her advisor. Often this can be beneficial for daughters in later life.

Older sons and daughters may not respond in the same way. Some will become distant or evasive, feeling unable to take on the role of confidant. Both boys and girls will feel a sense of concern and protectiveness towards their mothers, but each will respond differently.

When their mother commences a new relationship with another man, sons will often feel pushed to the periphery, often leading to behavioural issues, while daughters will be more likely to accept a stepfather and be able to have a meaningful relationship with him. Statistically, daughters of divorce are more likely to marry and have children early[58], or give birth before marriage, than children from non-divorced families.

Reconciling Parents to Children

Parents of broken families come under heavy stress during a relationship breakdown, as they go through a grieving process. They may experience stress during a move, legal proceedings, and need to maintain employment. The emotional needs of their children can be overlooked, or demoted down a long list of things all competing for attention.

Fathers Towards Children

When a father-child relationship shifts from family life to limited access after separation, it moves onto shaky ground. A father's role often becomes hazy – how does he discipline a child when he is unclear on both his own authority and responsibility within the new family unit? No longer involved in the day-to-day goings on of his children, a father can feel quickly distanced from his children's lives.

Courts, mothers and children assume that a father will maintain close contact afterwards, but this is often not the case. A father-child relationship is a complex tangle of interactions and emotions, which can often suffer critical wounds through the trauma of divorce. Many good men will distance themselves after a divorce, despite their desire to remain involved and close to their children due to painful feelings of guilt and regret. As many men are incapable of adequately dealing with their emotions and feelings of loss, bitterness and hurt, they'll find shame and meeting them at every interaction with their children. The way a lot of men deal with these emotions is to run - avoiding the issue to minimise the pain with infrequent, short visits despite their desire for meaningful interactions with their kids. It can be easier to cut and run, with the hope of moving on with a new family.

As a child grows, a father's pain can transform into acute loss as they see how much the child has grown at each subsequent meeting, especially more so where his ex-wife adapts well to the divorce. Men have well-earned reputation for being less competent at expressing their feelings. If you are a father who is experiencing ongoing regret or guilt as a result of your failings in this regard, you might want to re-read the section on processing guilt and regret.

Mothers Towards Children

In the wake of a father's absence, responsibility for everything falls on the mother. Chores, breadwinning, counselling, family management, planning and discipline all fall to the mother. This is usually an extremely heavy burden. Many might consider fleeing these responsibilities, and some do.

Married couples with children tend to be considered wealthier when compared with about 35 to 40 per cent of single-mother families[59]. Children who grow up living in an intact household with both biological parents present seem to do better on average, than children who grow up in single-parent households[60]. If you are a single mother, you may regret not being able to offer your children all that life had to offer. Perhaps it was music lessons, extra maths coaching, university, or regular holidays. If you did it on your own, your children probably missed out on a number of things. They may in turn begrudge you for this as they're growing up. Perhaps you are sorry you couldn't be there for them emotionally, as you were working through your own baggage. You may wish you could have been able to provide them with the benefits of a stable father figure.

It's time to look at letting go of the past, and reconciling with the present. Forgive the parties involved (including yourself), and do your best with what you have now.

Chapter 10 Exercises

1. Do you think you have room to improve in your manner when dealing with conflict? Where and in what situations?

2. What do you think about pride? What are the good and bad aspects of it in your life? Where is it useful, where does it get in the way?

3. Did you grow up with a divorce or separation in your family? How did you relate to your father? How did you relate to your mother?

4. In the course of applying the lessons in this book, have you noticed changes in:
The way you feel
The decisions you make
The reactions you have
The way you engage with people
The way your body functions (stress, sleep etc.)
Other symptoms

5. How successful have you been in using the motivation and reasons you set out in Chapter 1 to keep reading? What could you have done better? What would you have changed?

6. How would you rate yourself now in regard to each of the below categories (1 being low, 10 being high).

Anger
Guilt/shame
Fear
Optimism
Empathy
Self Confidence and Self-esteem
Anxiety
Physical Health
Romantic relationships
Compassion for others
Closeness of friendships

Look back at Chapter 2. Have there been improvements as you have read the book?

Going forward, what areas of your life do you plan to do differently?

Conclusion

A while back, I came across an article[61] by Bonnie Ware, author of the book 'The Top Five Regrets of the Dying'[62]. Bonnie worked with patients with serious medical illnesses; most of the time she witnessed people in the last one to three months of their lives. During this time, she found that in the final days of their lives the vast majority shared five common regrets.

1. I wish I'd had the courage to live a life true to myself, not the life others expected of me.
2. I wish I didn't work so hard.
3. I wish I'd had the courage to express my feelings.
4. I wish I had stayed in touch with my friends.
5. I wish that I had let myself be happier.

I want you to imagine you have a few days to live. Take a second and ask yourself each of these five questions. Knowing what you know about how to forgive and reconcile, how would you have lived your life differently? Is there a relationship you would like to fix? You may think that you have years left, but what if you didn't? We live our lives putting off life, putting off pain (and gain). I hope you start living life for today, and using that as motivation to work through things you've found too hard before.

Love is the ultimate goal. If you can trust, you can expose your heart enough to love again.

Unless we learn to wear our hearts on our sleeves, instead of behind a suit of armour, love won't get in, or at least not very far. When our walls are up we can't let love in even if we want to.

The more we can love, the more people will reciprocate and return the same warmth. As we come to discover that we're loved, valued, appreciated, and naturally worth loving, we'll find it easier to forgive other parties, and ourselves.

Learning that you're lovable is the key that will unlock your heart. Forgiveness is the first step in this process. My hope is that in reading and applying this book now, at the end of your life you'll be able to look back and answer these five questions with peace in your heart.

I wrote this book to give away and spread the knowledge of forgiveness. Once you've read it, I ask you to think of one or more people you could give it away to. If you want to help your friends, this book is designed to be run in a book group. All you need is a minimum of two copies, and you can run one.

If you have any feedback, either a testimony, or constructive criticism, I'd love to hear it. You can send me an email to mykey@mykeyrobinson.com.

References

Chapter 1

[1] *http://www.apa.org/international/resources/forgiveness.pdf*

[2] *Radhi H. Al-Mabuk, Robert D. Enright & Paul A. Cardis (1995). Forgiveness Education with Parentally Love-Deprived Late Adolescents. Journal of Moral Education 24 (4):427-444.*

[3] *http://www.nimh.nih.gov/statistics/index.shtml*

[4] *http://jama.jamanetwork.com/article.aspx?articleid=198847*

Chapter 2

[5] *Enright, R. D., & Fitzgibbons, R. P. (2000). Helping clients forgive: An empirical guide for resolving anger and restoring hope (pp. 65-88; 267-276). Washington, DC: APA*

[6] *Forgiveness as an intervention goal with incest survivors. By Freedman, Suzanne R.; Enright, Robert D. Journal of Consulting and Clinical Psychology, Vol 64(5), Oct 1996, 983-992.*

[7] *http://www.merriam-webster.com/dictionary/forgive*

[8] *Gordon, K.C., Hughes, F. M., Tomcik, N. B., Dixon, L. J., & Litzinger, S. (2009). Widening circles of impact: The effects of forgiveness on family functioning. Journal of Family Psychology, 23, 1-13.*

[9] *Freedman, Suzanne R.; Enright, Robert D Forgiveness as an intervention goal with incest survivors. Journal of Consulting and Clinical Psychology, Vol 64(5), Oct 1996, 983-992*

[10] *.Kanz, Jason E (2000), How Do People Conceptualize and Use Forgiveness? The Forgiveness Attitudes Questionnaire, Counseling & Values;Apr2000, Vol. 44 Issue 3, p174*

[11] *Braithwaite SR, Selby EA, Fincham FD. Forgiveness and relationship satisfaction: mediating mechanisms. J Fam Psychol. 2011 Aug;25(4):551-9.*

[12] *Mullet, E., Houdbine, A., Laumonier, S., & Girard, M. (1998). "Forgiveness": Factor structure in a sample of young, middle-aged, and elderly adults. European Psychologist, 3, 289–297*

Chapter 3

[13] *Radhi H. Al-Mabuk, Robert D. Enright & Paul A. Cardis (1995). Forgiveness Education with Parentally Love-Deprived Late Adolescents. Journal of Moral Education 24 (4):427-444.*

[14] *Hamermesh , D.S & Biddle, J.   Beauty and the Labor Market, The American Economic Review, Vol. 84, No. 5, (Dec., 1994), pp. 1174-1194*

[15] *http://www.un.org/en/documents/udhr/index.shtml*

[16] *Mullet, E., Houdbine, A., Laumonier, S., & Girard, M. (1998). "Forgiveness": Factor structure in a sample of young, middle-aged, and elderly adults. European Psychologist, 3, 289–297*

[17] *Mullet, E., Houdbine, A., Laumonier, S., & Girard, M. (1998). "Forgiveness": Factor structure in a sample of young, middle-aged, and elderly adults. European Psychologist, 3, 289–297*

[18] *Frank D. Fincham, F. Georgia Paleari, Camillo Regalia, Forgiveness in marriage: The role of relationship quality, attributions, and empathy Personal Relationships (2002), pp. 27-37,*

[19] A. F. Shariff and A. Norenzayan; God Is Watching You: Priming God Concepts Increases Prosocial Behavior in an Anonymous Economic Game; Psychological Science *September 2007* vol. 18 no. 9 *803-809*

[21] Andrew Newberg, M.D., Mark Robert Waldman (2010). How God Changes Your Brain, Breakthrough Findings from a Leading Neuroscientist. Random House

[22] Exline JJ, Baumeister RF, Bushman BJ, Campbell WK, Finkel EJ. Too proud to let go: narcissistic entitlement as a barrier to forgiveness. J Pers Soc Psychol. 2004 Dec;87(6):894-912.

[23] Wohl, M. J. A., & Branscombe, N. R. (2005). Forgiveness and collective guilt assignment to historical perpetrator groups depend on level of social category inclusiveness. Journal of Personality and Social Psychology, 88, 288-303.

Chapter 4
[24] http://www.muskingum.edu/~psych/psycweb/history/watson.htm

[25] Wilkowski, B M.; Robinson, M D.; Troop-Gordon, W; How does cognitive control reduce anger and aggression? The role of conflict monitoring and forgiveness processes; Journal of Personality and Social Psychology, Vol 98(5), May 2010, 830-840. doi:

[26] http://www.merriam-webster.com/dictionary/rumination

Chapter 5

[27] The Hour - Aug 6, 1991 http://news.google.com/newspapers?nid=1916&dat=19910806&id=DQ8hAAAAIBAJ&sjid=knYFAAAAIBAJ&pg=3451,721666

[28] Exline, J.J., Baumeister, R.F., Zell, A.L., Kraft, A., & Witvliet, C.V.O. (2008). Not so innocent: Does seeing one's own capability for wrongdoing predict forgiveness? Journal of Personality and Social Psychology, 94,495-515.

[30] Exline JJ, Baumeister RF, Bushman BJ, Campbell WK, Finkel EJ. Too proud to let go: narcissistic entitlement as a barrier to forgiveness. J Pers Soc Psychol. 2004 Dec;87(6):894-912 and McCullough, M. E., & Witvliet, C. V. O. (2002). The psychology of forgiveness. In C. R. Snyder & S. Lopez (Eds.), Handbook of Positive Psychology (pp. 446–458). New York: Oxford University Press

[31] Exline, J. J., Worthington, E. L., Jr., Hill, P., & McCullough, M. E. (2003). Forgiveness and justice: A research agenda for social and personality psychology. Personality and Social Psychology Review, 7, 337–348.

[32] Finkelhor, D., & Browne, A. (1985). The traumatic impact of child sexual abuse: A conceptualization. American Journal of Orthopsychiatry, 55, 530–541.

[33] Alexander P. (1993). The differential effects of abuse characteristics and attachment in the prediction of long-term effects of sexual abuse. Journal of Interpersonal Violence, 8, 346-362.

[34] Rempel, J.K.; Ross M; Holmes, J G , Trust and communicated attributions in close relationships. Journal of Personality and Social Psychology, Vol 81(1), Jul 2001, 57-64

[35] McCullough ME, Luna LR, Berry JW, Tabak BA, Bono G. On the form and function of forgiving: modeling the time-forgiveness relationship and testing the valuable relationships hypothesis. Emotion. 2010 Jun;10(3):358-76.

[36] http://en.wikipedia.org/wiki/Repressed_memory

Chapter 6

[37] Kyle D. Pruett, M.D.; Yale Child Study Centre, New Haven, Connecticut; Zero to Three Journal, August/September 1997 (Vol. 18:1)

[38] *http://www.dol.gov/wb/factsheets/Qf-nursing.htm*
http://nces.ed.gov/fastfacts/display.asp?id=28

[39] *Broude, G. J. (1990). Protest masculinity: A further look at the causes and the concept. Ethos, 18(1), 103-122.*

[40] *Stifter C.A., Grant, W; Infant responses to frustration: Individual differences in the expression of negative affect.*
JOURNAL OF NONVERBAL BEHAVIOR Volume 17, Number 3 (1993), 187-204

[41] *Blakeslee, S., & Wallerstein, J. S. (1989). Second chances: Men, women and children a decade after divorce. New York:*
Ticknor & Fields.

[42] *Blakeslee, S., & Wallerstein, J. S. (1989). Second chances: Men, women and children a decade after divorce. New York:*
Ticknor & Fields.

Chapter 7

[43] *Fincham FD, Hall JH, Beach SRH. Forgiveness in marriage: Current status and future directions. Family*
Relations. 2006;55:415–427.

[45] *Sternberg, R. (1986). "A Triangular Theory of Love." Psychological Review. 93(2),119-35.*
Sternberg, R. & Gracek, S. (1984). "The Nature of Love." Journal of Personality and Social Psychology. 4 (2), 312-29.

[46] *http://plato.stanford.edu/entries/laws-of-nature/*

[47] *http://www.lhc.ac.uk/*

Chapter 8

[48] *Lerner, J. S., & Keltner, D. (2000). Beyond valence: Toward a model of emotion specific influences on judgment and*
choice. Cognition and Emotion, 14, 473-493.

[49] *Dutton, D. G., & Painter, S. (1993). Emotional attachments in abusive relationships: A test of traumatic bonding*
theory. Violence and Victims, 8(2), 105-120.

[50] *Finkel, Rusbult, Kumashiro, & Hannon, 2002, The Effect: When Forgiving Erodes Self-Respect and Self-Concept*
Clarity, Journal of Personality and Social Psychology

Chapter 9

[51] *Baumeister, R.F., & Exline, J.J. (2000). Self-control, morality, and human strength. Journal of Social and Clinical*
Psychology, 19, 29-42.

[52] *The Hiding Place (1971), Corrie Ten Boom, John Sherrill, Elizabeth Sherrill, Baker Publishing Group*

Chapter 10

[53] *McCullough, M.E., Fincham, F.D., & Tsang, J. (2003). Forgiveness, forbearance, and time: The temporal unfolding of*
transgression-related interpersonal motivations. Journal of Personality and Social Psychology, 84, 540-557.

[54] *Santelli AG, Struthers CW, Eaton J., Fit to forgive: Exploring the interaction between regulatory focus, repentance, and*
forgiveness. J Pers Soc Psychol. 2009 Feb;96(2):381-94.

[55] *Blakeslee, S., & Wallerstein, J. S. (1989). Second chances: Men, women and children a decade after divorce. New York:*
Ticknor & Fields.

[56] *Robert D. Hess and Kathleen A. Post-Divorce Family Relationships as Mediating Factors in the Consequences of Divorce for Children Camara Journal of Social Issues, v35 n4 p79-96 Fall 1979*

[57] *Blakeslee, S., & Wallerstein, J. S. (1989). Second chances: Men, women and children a decade after divorce. New York: Ticknor & Fields.*

[58] *http://www.nber.org/digest/feb01/w7968.html*

[59] *http://www.mdrc.org/publications/386/testimony.html*

[60] *McLanahan, S., & Sandefur, G. D. (1994). Growing up with a single parent: What hurts, what helps. Cambridge, Mass.: Harvard University Press*

[61] *http://www.huffingtonpost.com/bronnie-ware/top-5-regrets-of-the-dyin_b_1220965.html*

[62] *The Top Five Regrets of the Dying: A Life Transformed by the Dearly Departing, Bronnie Ware, Hay House; (2012)*

Printed in Great Britain
by Amazon